THE
CHRISTIAN
TEACHER

THE
CHRISTIAN
TEACHER

Perry LeFevre

ABINGDON PRESS
NEW YORK • NASHVILLE

THE CHRISTIAN TEACHER

Copyright © MCMLVIII by Abingdon Press

Library of Congress Catalog Card Number: 58-10460

SET UP, PRINTED, AND BOUND BY THE
PARTHENON PRESS, AT NASHVILLE,
TENNESSEE, UNITED STATES OF AMERICA

TO

The Danforth Foundation

The Faculty Christian Fellowship

The Hazen Foundation

The National Council on Religion in Higher Education

Pioneers in the renaissance
of religion in American higher education

PREFACE

In 1892 WILLIAM JAMES WAS ASKED BY THE HARVARD CORPORA-
tion to give public lectures to a group of teachers on the
subject of psychology. This request came at a time when
new developments in psychology were evoking considerable
popular interest and when psychology was being taken with
increasing seriousness by the teaching profession. James's
lectures appeared in 1899 as a small book entitled *Talks to
Teachers*. In their published form these "talks" reached a
wider audience, stimulating discussion and thought among
many teachers throughout the English-speaking world.
Today we live in a time of revived interest and concern both
for education and for religious values. In the last quarter
century there has been a renaissance of religion in American higher education. The climate of our institutions of
higher learning has been changing. Teachers and administrators are becoming increasingly aware of the philosophical and religious dimensions of the educational issues which
confront them. More and more of them are beginning to
probe the relationship between their own faith and their
responsibilities in higher education. Still others who have

no firm religious commitment have become willing to examine the Christian option and take it seriously. At the same time and increasingly in recent years the American public has been confronted with a crisis in American higher education. The tremendous increase in student enrollments, the shortage of teachers, the undermining of the financial security of our colleges and universities through inflation, as well as the impact of cold war, have focused attention on the whole educational enterprise in America as never before. A lively discussion has been stimulated throughout our colleges and universities as well as in the public press concerning the nature and goals of higher education.

The following chapters are intended to speak to this new situation in higher education. In a way they are "talks to Christian teachers." They contain some of the things I would like to say if I could sit down with groups of Christian teachers or with those who are concerned with both teaching and the Christian faith in our colleges and universities. They are meant to be informal, and their aim and scope are limited. The aim of this work is limited in the sense that it is intended to be suggestive and exploratory. I would hope that what I have said may provoke an interest, stir up thought and discussion, and move individual teachers and administrators to consider their work in a new light or from a new perspective. Only such a hope and intention has led me beyond my professional competence as a theologian to venture into such areas as the humanities, the social sciences, and the physical and biological sciences to deal with issues which might more properly be held to be the business of teachers and specialists within these fields. The scope of this brief work is limited as well. I have concentrated on certain issues in the area of teaching and learning. I have not intended to give an exhaustive or inclusive treatment of issues or answers even in this area, still less to produce a fully developed philosophy or theology of higher education. What I have written, however, might be thought of as a contribution to a developing Christian theology of education.

The subject of the following chapters centers around two questions: What are the Christian teacher's concerns in higher education? What difference does it make in an individual's teaching if he takes both his teaching and his Christian faith seriously? In one way or another all of the chapters are woven around these two central questions. The fundamental thesis is that the distinguishing mark of the Christian teacher is his sense of calling. He is called to be a Christian, but to exercise that calling within a particular profession. His sense of calling will affect all that he does as a teacher: his handling of his own discipline, his concern for teaching method, his interest in understanding the student, his conception of his role as counselor, the part he plays in his college or university community, and his interpretation of the teaching-learning process. The individual chapters are explications of this thesis. They are attempts to clarify some of the specific ways in which the Christian teacher may fulfill his sense of calling within his profession.

I would like to thank Kenneth Brown of the Danforth Foundation for inviting me to deliver a series of lectures on Christian teaching at the First Danforth Teachers Conference at Camp Miniwanca, an invitation which was the occasion for the initial statement of some of the thoughts contained within this book. Dr. Brown has kindly given me his critical comments on a first draft of this material. My gratitude is also extended to colleagues, students, and friends who have heard or read parts of this work. Their comments have been helpful. I am indebted to my wife for her careful criticism of style and form of expression.

PERRY LEFEVRE

CONTENTS

Chapter I

THE VOCATION OF THE CHRISTIAN TEACHER

WHAT IS THE DISTINCTION BETWEEN A GOOD TEACHER AND A good Christian teacher? This is the issue which arises more and more frequently in what seems to be a renaissance of faculty interest in the Christian faith. The question is not an easy one to answer if we approach it solely from the point of view of the nature of good teaching, and then ask whether a teacher's being a Christian adds anything to the quality of his teaching. We all know of excellent teachers who would not call themselves Christians just as we know Christian teachers whose teaching is not particularly good. A more fruitful approach is needed, for the ultimate criteria for any profession are not internal to the profession itself. They are related to what the individual or the group holds to be most important, to what is believed to be the final meaning or significance of life itself. From the Christian point of view this is another way of saying that the ultimate criteria are theological. Theological criteria for a profession can be elaborated through the Christian doctrine of vocation.

Christians are "called"; they are called to the Christian life, to a Christian vocation in a larger sense, at the same time that they may feel themselves to be called to some specialized vocation such as law, medicine, preaching, or teaching. A particular profession can be a calling from God only because it is possible to exercise the more general calling, that of living the Christian life, within it. Logically, though perhaps not chronologically, we are Christians first and Christian teachers or businessmen second. This is because our religious interest or concern is our ultimate concern. All other concerns are relative or even instrumental. Should we feel that we could no longer be Christians within our particular profession or that we could better exercise our responsibility as Christians within another calling, other things being equal, we would feel a strong inward pressure to relinquish our present work and to seek some other.

The Christian vocation in the larger sense, the living of the Christian life, takes its meaning from the concrete situation in which we find ourselves as men and women. What is this concrete situation? What is the gospel which speaks to it, which illuminates it, interpreting it and giving man a directive for action within it? A large part of the human situation can be described in words of wonder, joy, and gratitude. There is much which makes life good to most of us much of the time. There is the joy of family life deeply shared, the laughter and happiness of children, the comfort of home, the pleasures of friendship. There is the wonder of the beauty of nature: trees and flowers, mountains and lakes, cloud and sun. There is our own sense of well-being when we are in good health or doing needful work. There are the countless gifts which merit gratitude—food, clothing, knowledge. The treasures of human creativity in art, music, and literature preserved in our cultural heritage; the ideals of freedom, justice, and brotherhood; the structures of social, political, and economic life which make possible the ordered pursuit of human activities, are great goods in human life. All of this and much more would have to be said in a balanced presentation of the human situation. Though these positive elements are of enormous importance for man, they are not in fact what makes the human situation a human predicament. If these factors in man's life represented the whole of his existence, religions of salvation and redemption like the Christian faith would be irrelevant. We might still celebrate man's dependence on God the Creator, but the whole redemptive thrust of God's historical activity in Jesus Christ would be uncalled for, meaningless. It is because the human situation is also a predicament, because evil is mixed with the good in human life, that the message of Jesus Christ is a gospel, a good news, for it is the message of the redemption of man. We need then to turn to the darker side of the human situation, to those universal human experiences which make a redemptive message relevant and God's redemptive acts a gospel.

What is the human predicament? My own understanding of this darker side of human existence may not make for very pleasant reading, but it may give readers pause for thought. It may move one to make his own analysis and interpretation. When I look out upon the world, it appears to me as a world in which there is an enormous amount of hatred. Sometimes the enormity of the hatred in the world almost overwhelms me, for it exists on the international level, the intergroup level, and the interpersonal level. This fact is almost too obvious to elaborate. It ranges all the way from active and aggressive warfare and the struggle for power, through the bitter prejudices of race and class, to the outward expression and inner feelings of personal hostility and ill will. Sometimes the centrifugal forces which thrust man from man, group from group, and nation from nation seem to be consciously controlled and intended by man. At other times we seem grasped by powers which are out of hand, sweeping us into a holocaust which none of us wills or desires.

Such hatred leads almost inevitably to injury. The consequence of these centrifugal forces, intended or unintended, is that people get hurt; groups get hurt; nations get hurt. The hurt is not only physical and material as in the case of outward acts of aggression; attitudes and feelings of hostility produce inner misery and suffering at all these levels. They tincture the very atmosphere. They poison our environment. They prevent the emergence of new goods and the realization of many of the creative possibilities latent in the human situation. All of us have experienced this. All of us have known it as both spectators and participants.

The world I see seems to me to be a world permeated by doubt. Doubt is essentially lack of trust. And where there are hatred and injury, it is easy to see why people and groups and nations will not trust one another. When a labor union has felt the hatred and nearly been crushed by a managing group, when a racial minority has had its homes bombed and its members humiliated, when an individual has been attacked physically or psychologically or has had his confidence betrayed, how can there be trust? The doubt is not only intellectual, in the sense that we do not know what to believe. It also exists at the feeling level. We don't know whom to believe. We don't know whom or what to trust. Trust has been so often betrayed that we hesitate to trust other nations, other groups, persons within our own group, or even ourselves. This issue of trust comes close to the very center of religion, for it can finally lead to raising the basic theological question: What *is* ultimately trustworthy? It is a question which Job must have faced. It has been man's question through all generations. What, when everything upon which man has based his trust proves to be undependable, can man finally trust? This is not just a question prompted by intellect or feeling. It is raised by a man in his wholeness. For most of us it is not raised as sharply as it was for Job, but it is the question which runs through every particular doubt and every particular failure of trust.

When lack of trust has proceeded far enough or when a basic trust has never been present at all, there is *despair*. As long as some kind of trust remains, there is hope. Despair is that condition in which hope deserts us. There are many people without hope in our world. There are many times when hope deserts all of us. Despair comes in the midst of suffering unless, preserved somewhere in the inner man, there remains an element of trust. How much hope can there be for the person or the nation or the group which has lost all upon which it has depended?

Sometimes when I consider how man spends his days, it seems as if a pall of darkness had come over his world. There is the darkness of misunderstanding. Like all the characteristics of the human situation, this misunderstanding is found at the international, the intergroup, and the interpersonal levels. We all have blind spots in our under-

17

standing of the lives of others; none of us can share fully
the hopes and fears, the joys and sorrows, of another.
But there are degrees and kinds of misunderstanding.
Sometimes there seems to be an unconscious desire to misunderstand and misinterpret the meanings and the behavior
of other groups, nations, and persons. Beyond misunderstanding there is simple ignorance. We do not know what
we might know. Ignorance is not just inertia. It may be the
result of lack of opportunity or of someone's conscious
effort to keep us ignorant. Beyond ignorance there lies the
realm of distortion and lies. There are vast forces in our
public life seeking to distort the truth for their own interests. There are subtle forces in personal life and in ourselves, disclosed when we see ourselves clearly enough,
which twist and turn the truth or exploit the ignorance and
misunderstanding of man in full conscious awareness and
with malice aforethought.

Finally, as I look out upon the human situation, I see a
world marked by sadness. Human life is full of tragedy.
Life is a vast mixture of good and evil. I have walked
through the great cities, looked into people's faces, overheard their conversations, and asked myself : How much joy,
how much happiness, is there in the life of man? Faces and
conversation, the lives of men and women in unguarded
moments, betray them. Not the slum dwellers alone but the
Gold Coast and the suburb have their sadness and despair.
Perhaps the brokenness of human life is most accessible to
those who know the inner lives of families and individuals
most intimately. The family physician, the minister, the
social worker, or the observant inhabitant of the small town
comes to know the darker side of human life as well as anyone. I have lived in such close proximity to other folk and

have known the heavy burdens they carry. Walking down a village street, one can point them out.

Here is a home in which there is a broken mind, a loved family member for whom the strain and stress of life was too much, whose inner balance finally gave way. We all know something of the sorrow and suffering such experience brings to those intimately involved even if we have no knowledge of the experience on its inward side. Here again is a home in which there is a broken family—marital discord, family tension, rising to the breaking point. We know what this does to the children, to the larger family, to the community, and to the participants themselves. Or there is a house in which there is a body broken by accident or disease. Again we may know the many many homes in which there are broken hearts: hearts broken by defeated expectations—whether of love, of success, of material recognition, of reputation. Lives lived full of regret and reservation; all of the possibilities that might have been but for one reason or another can be no more.

Finally there is the brokenness which no one of us escapes. "Blest be the tie that binds," but ties that bind can be and are broken, whether they are ties of friendship, of marriage, of children to parents and parents to children, of loved ones to one another. Friends move away; children leave home; loved ones die. No one of us escapes either our own death or the experience of the breaking of human ties by death. This is a world of hatred, injury, doubt, despair, darkness, and sadness. Such is the human predicament.

Yet in the midst of such a world, in the midst of this human situation, if you are sensitive, you can see, and feel, and know, the ongoing reclamation of life, its renewal, and its redemption. In the midst of all of the threats to fulfill-

19

ment we see situations in which life is nourished, sustained, and fulfilled. Sometimes this can be seen in and through large-scale events. The historical writers of the Old Testament saw it there. But international struggles, even those among the lesser masses of men, are exceedingly complex. They are the heaping together of all of the complexities of individual life and interpersonal relations. Perhaps nowhere more clearly can the nature of this reclaiming, nourishing, sustaining, redeeming power be seen than in personal and interpersonal life itself.

How would you characterize the working of sources of redemption and nourishment and fulfillment which reach beyond and may run counter to the intention and direction of man? How would you name that which alone seems to be able to transmute tragedy and bring the best that can be out of a situation? How would you describe that which can raise life in many circumstances from mere endurance or defeat to renewal and worth? In what terms would you speak of that in man which makes it possible for him to aid in this process? How would you describe the behavior of one who made this his vocation in life?

Christians have had answers to these questions. The Christian understanding of life is a gospel because Christians have known and understood and felt that in the midst of all the threats to man's life—the hatred, injury, doubt, despair, the darkness and the tragic character of human existence—there was a power for salvation, for fulfillment, for the transmutation, if not the abolition, of tragedy. The love which the first Christians saw in Christ became for them the ground for understanding this power which overcomes tragedy, which brings healing, which nourishes and sustains man even in a tragic world. And the Christian vocation became a ministry in his name of the active expression of this love. Like them, we are called to be instruments of God's action, to be channels of his love. We are called not so much to speak the gospel in words as to demonstrate it in our lives. The vocation of the Christian man is the reclamation of the human situation, the renewing of life, the redemption of the tragic character of existence, the mutual ministry of reconciliation to all men. His prayer is the prayer of Francis of Assisi:

> Lord, make me an instrument of thy peace.
> Where there is hatred, let me sow love;
> Where there is injury, pardon;
> Where there is discord, union;
> Where there is doubt, faith;
> Where there is despair, hope;
> Where there is darkness, light;
> Where there is sadness, joy.

> O divine Master, grant that I may not so much
>   seek to be consoled as to console,
> To be understood as to understand,
> To be loved as to love;
> For it is in giving that we receive,
> It is in pardoning that we are pardoned,
> And it is in dying that we are born to eternal life.

If this is one way of stating the meaning of Christian vocation, it is also a way of stating the vocation of the Christian teacher, and the prayer of Francis of Assisi may well be taken as a Christian teacher's prayer. Teaching for the Christian is a ministry, just as is any other particular Christian vocation. Teaching is a specialized form of the general Christian vocation. The question with which we started then becomes sharply focused. How is this general Christian vocation to be channeled or expressed in the particular vocation of the teacher? To be a Christian teacher is not simply to be a good teacher. It is not simply to be a teacher and a Christian. It is rather to express one's Christian vocation in one's teaching. To put the matter this way places all one's questions about teaching in a new context. It places them in the context of ultimate concern and commitment. It puts the subsidiary questions into the same context. The teacher's concern with his methods of teaching, with his subject matter, with the student, with his various roles in relation to the academic situation and the community, needs then to be refocused.

This position which I have so briefly stated seems to me to be subject to both misunderstanding and criticism from several sides. On the one hand there are those who honestly believe that the Christian teacher ought to try to convert his students to the Christian faith, that it is his obligation as a Christian to state the faith and doctrine persuasively, perhaps even evangelistically, wherever possible. On the other hand there are those, both Christians and secularists, who believe that such teaching so violates the integrity of the teaching process and of the student himself that, if the teacher has a faith or is a Christian, he must keep his faith and his teaching separate. Both of these positions imply an understanding of the Christian faith which I do not accept. My own point of view begins with the assumption that each of us tries to make whatever sense he can out of his own experience of life, to discover for himself what is to be his ultimate concern or what is finally trustworthy. Such ultimate concern or final trust expresses itself in all of the multifarious concerns or values the individual has, including his profession or vocation. The Christian faith is not a systematic doctrinal interpretation of life, though it may well include such. It is primarily a way of relating oneself to the events of life, a way of apprehending these events, of responding to them as a whole person. It is the expression of a kind of personhood. It includes one's feeling response to life as well as his intellectual understanding of life.

The implication of this view of the Christian faith is that faith cannot be a matter of indoctrination. Doctrine, or intellectual understanding, is only a part of the Christian faith. It is hardly the essential part, since one can certainly be a simple Christian without a clear theological understanding of the faith. Moreover, some of us at least believe that it is possible to formulate the intellectual understanding of the faith in more than one way. Though the Christian faith often requires theological understanding, the simple transformation of the faith into a set of intellectual propositions about the world and man is a misunderstanding and a distortion of it. Nor can the Christian faith understood as I have described it be a matter for subtle forms of coercion. The Christian life and the Christian faith must by its very nature be a free response. You cannot force people into the Christian mold. The Christian life is defined by acts of freedom. Such acts can issue only from a responsible self. Not only can you not coerce individual acts of love or forgiveness, but you cannot force the development of the kind of person who is capable of love and forgiveness, of spreading trust, hope, and joy. People do not become Christians in this fashion. Even if a teacher could persuasively create a willingness and a desire in his students to become such persons, this would not suffice. One does not become this kind of person simply by willing it or striving for it. The universal Christian testimony is that such transformation is beyond one's own control and will. One becomes such a person, to the degree that he does become one, only in response to God's own judgment and love, whether this love is mediated through other persons, the church, or through a confrontation with the life and teachings of Christ. It is not in the power of the teacher to bring this about. If such transformation happens in part because of him, it happens because God acts in and through him.

Commitment, then, to the Christian faith on the teacher's part does not imply indoctrination and does not threaten the integrity of the student or of the teaching process. It does imply, however, that the Christian teacher's faith and his teaching cannot be kept separate from each other. Inasmuch as he feels himself called to teaching as a Christian vocation, he feels himself called to a life of love, pardon, trust, hope, light, joy. He is not merely called to perform acts of love, forgiveness, to increase trust, hope, and joy; he is called to be the kind of person for whom such acts are the natural expression of his own personhood. Being this kind of person cannot be separated from the way in which he pursues any of his tasks. It will necessarily interpenetrate every aspect of his professional activity. What is important is that this interpenetration be acknowledged and critically understood. So understood it will be impossible to countenance poor teaching or the neglect of one's particular subject matter for the sake of some vague communication of religious values. The Christian teacher may or may not be a great teacher, but he will be the best teacher he can be. To be a Christian teacher is to take one's teaching with pre-eminent seriousness. It is to accept it as a trust, a call from God.

Another issue which may be raised needs seriously to be considered. Some will say: "But may not a good secular teacher with a real concern for his students take the Francis of Assisi prayer as his guide? May he not be so moved by humanitarian impulses that he tries to treat the students in the same way that a Christian teacher might? What then is the distinguishing character of the Christian teacher's work?" This question must be addressed again and again in various ways by both the reader and the writer throughout this book. A beginning answer may be made here. Granted the possibility that a sensitive non-Christian might behave toward his students, relate himself to colleagues, the college community, and his subject matter in ways dictated by the pattern symbolized in Francis' prayer, or even that he might in his own person be the kind of individual for whom such behavior was the natural expression of his character, what then? Behind such similar behavior patterns and character structures there would lie essential differences of understanding, experience, and motivation. To put the difference most succinctly, the Christian's vocation is experienced as a "call." It is not the result of a self-imposed task, nor solely his reaction to a rational analysis of life. The Christian's understanding of himself and his world as well as his motivation is grounded in Christ. In whatever way such grounding takes place, and there are many ways, the reference point for meaning is his own experience of Christ. It is this, with all that it implies, that differentiates the Christian from the non-Christian. The first Christians came to their understanding of the world and of God through Christ. They came to a new relationship to the world and to God through Christ. In the midst of all of the threats to man's life, in the face of the tragic character of human existence, they came to understand and feel the power for salvation, for fulfillment, and for the transmutation if not the abolition of tragedy through their encounter with Christ. They found themselves in the hands of a power not their own, of an otherness which spoke to them in their situation, which grasped them and drew them beyond themselves, remaking them in its own image and likeness, empowering them for their life in the world. Something of this initiating experience, whatever forms it may take and whatever interpretations may be given to it, informs the life, the vocation, and the work of the committed Christian teacher. The meaning of the Christian teacher's vocation is framed within a different stream of experience. His self-understanding finds its illumination in Christ. He feels dependent on and empowered for what he is and does by One who stands beyond him as well as in him, by One who is behind him impelling him forward and ahead of him luring him on. He not only accepts his vocation as a trust from God, as something holy, but he knows that in this trust he is not alone. He knows, too, that he is not his own.

Chapter II

THE CHRISTIAN TEACHER
AND HIS DISCIPLINE

THE THESIS HAS BEEN ADVANCED THAT THERE IS A REAL DIFFER-
ence between a committed Christian teacher and secular
teacher. This difference centers in the Christian teacher's
sense of vocation. His profession is a calling—from God.
He accepts it as a trust. For the Christian, teaching cannot
be just another job. He not only will take his teaching with
pre-eminent seriousness, but somehow all of his responsibilities as a teacher will be focused in a special way. They
will be seen from the perspective of ultimate concern and
commitment. That ultimate concern will be reflected in and
interpenetrate all his professional activities. He not only
will understand himself and the meaning of his work as a
teacher differently, but his interest in his own discipline,
his methods of teaching, the way in which he relates himself to students, his view of the life of the college or university community, will all be affected by his Christian vocation which he will try to express in and through his teaching.

At some points his behavior, observed objectively, may

not differ from that of his secular colleague, for good teaching is good teaching whoever does it. Certain subject matter must be dealt with in a given discipline no matter what the commitment of the teacher. Yet even here the motivation and the inner meaning of the teacher's actions may be very different. The Christian's motivation and self-understanding arise out of a different frame of reference. His interpretation of the meaning of what he is doing and why he is doing it are distinguishable from that of the non-Christian teacher. At other points the Christian teacher may differ markedly in his teaching from his secular colleagues, and differ not just because of personal idiosyncrasy but because he is a Christian. It is one of the purposes of the following chapters to indicate points at which these assertions are true.

At the forefront of many of the contemporary discussions of religion and higher education lies the question of the relation of the Christian teacher to his own discipline. Does the Christian teacher have some peculiar relationship to the subject matter of his own discipline which distinguishes him from his secular colleagues? How are the particular disciplines to be related to the Christian faith, and how are they related to one another in the light of the Christian faith? Such questions are being discussed around the country in conferences, in small local campus groups, in the Faculty Christian Fellowship. For many teachers, newly awakened to the fact that textbooks and courses often do not give a fair hearing to religion, the most important question concerns when and how it is legitimately possible to bring the discussion of religious material into the classroom. An attempt to answer this kind of query has been made in many of the Hazen pamphlets on religious perspectives in the various disciplines, now collected in book form under the title *Religious Perspectives in College Teaching*.[1] The writers of these pamphlets find a place for dealing with religious issues within their own disciplines because religion is an important part of that segment of life with which their discipline is concerned. This is true, for example, of sociology, psychology, literature, and music. In discussing the music of the Christian Era at least, religious questions can hardly be avoided since much western music has been written and used for religious purposes or to express religious convictions. The music cannot be understood apart from the religious context out of which it came. Just so the sociologist or historian or anthropologist has a legitimate opportunity and an important responsibility for discussing religion because religion is one of the basic social, historical, and cultural phenomena. The sociologist may want to show the place of religion in the social order, to depict its conservative and creative roles, to describe its origins in response to inescapable human needs, to show its involvement in the "deepest complexities of the human lot."[2] In his interest in communicating an understanding of other social phenomena, he will have to chart the impact of religious motivation, organization, and of the great cultural systems of values (largely derived from religious sources) on the life and interaction of groups within the structure of a given society. Thus he will find it legitimate and important to delineate Weber's thesis of the intimate connection of Protestantism and the development of capitalism; he will want the student to recognize the strong religious components in American social life, the predominant influence historically of "nonconformist" Protestantism, and the counterimpact of progressive secularization and of religious influences derived from different traditions.

The psychologist has a similar opportunity and a demand put upon him to understand the religious aspect of man's life, his religious experience, the sources and effects of his religious beliefs in personal life and development. When psychologists have dealt with religion, they have most often concerned themselves with the strange, the unusual, or the peripheral. It may be that such phenomena do shed light on the religious life of man, but much could be gained by an effort directed toward understanding the part religious belief and practice play in the lives of ordinary people. It may be, as psychologists like Robert B. MacLeod maintain, that such study would illuminate the psychologist's understanding of key problems within his discipline, such as those of cognitive structure, feeling and emotion, and motivation.[3] Apart from this it would help the student to comprehend the function and the value of religion in personal life and to come to some critical assessment of the truth of many of the religious claims as well as of the adequacy of many of the psychological theories which purport to explain human behavior.

In the field of literature and art, as in music, the religious dimension cannot be neglected. The creative work of the artist, the poet, the dramatist, the novelist, is shaped both by personal convictions and by the religious spirit of the age in which he worked. To study the literature, the art, or the music of a period without understanding the part played by the religious dimension of a culture or of the individual experience which produced it is to misunderstand it or to understand it incompletely. The literature and art of Western civilization, like the music, is permeated by the language and thought of religion, by religious feeling, by theological ideas. Who can pretend to understand Dante, or Milton, or T. S. Eliot, apart from an understanding of the religious culture which molded their thought and feeling or the personal religious pilgrimage which governs their perception of life and its meaning? Who can understand contemporary literature and art apart from the cultural crisis of our time, a crisis which reflects the dissolution of the binding power of the Christian myth? Or who can assess the new and creative cultural movements without acknowledging the "continuing operation of the biblical and Christian tradition in its obscure disguises in modern movements?" [4]

The Christian teacher will surely be moved to "play fair" with religion within his own discipline. Where there is the opportunity and where it is legitimate to introduce the study of religion within a given discipline, he will want to do so. What is communicated to the student through the neglect of the study of religion or of the religious dimension of a subject matter is that religion is unimportant in human life, or that while once important perhaps, it is no longer so. Through failure to be confronted by the most profound religious thought, the student may, like so many of his teachers, have his religious life and thinking arrested at their childhood level. Faced with the conflict between his childish understanding of the Christian faith and his more sophisticated understanding of other realms of knowledge and experience, he may reject the religious option altogether. Confrontation by more mature forms of religious life and thought is of great importance. At a time when he is capable of deeper intellectual understanding and has a growing range of experience of life, such confrontation may help him to maintain openness to the religious option. It may also provide him with the materials for responsible thinking about his own religious commitment.

Another way of approaching the problem of the relation of religion and the Christian faith to a particular discipline proceeds from the assumption that the unity of God and the universe implies the unity of all knowledge and truth. All truth is God's truth. In seeking truth about the world, man, culture, nature, we are studying God's truth. We are thinking his thoughts after him. As Professor Coulson writes in an excellent little book entitled *An Approach to Christian Education:*

> Each separate discipline of study, be it art or history or science, shows us something of the reality which is God. No one view shows us everything. The fullness of knowledge of God comes when we can place all separate revelations of Him side by side recognizing their differences and rejoicing in their complementary character, by which our knowledge of God becomes three-dimensional instead of two-dimensional as must inevitably be the case for any one view alone.[5]

Such a view has a long history. One of its direct ancestors is the classic on the relation of the Christian faith to university education, Newman's *The Idea of a University.* For Newman the matter is a little more complicated. He agrees with Coulson's dimensional or perspectival view of the knowledge gained through the particular disciplines. The different disciplines are so many different perspectives, each of them abstract and incomplete by itself. Knowledge is a whole, but each discipline is a fragmentary and disparate segment of the whole. Its truth is part of a larger unitive Truth. "All truths of whatever kind form into one large body of Truth, by virtue of the consistency between one truth and another, which is a connecting link running through them all.'' [6] Truth cannot contradict truth, though at any given moment from the human perspective there may be apparently irreconcilable conflicts among the disciplines. Thus we might say, and Newman himself uses a similar illustration, biology, psychology, sociology, cultural anthropology, theology and philosophy, physics and chemistry, each studies man from its own perspective. The truth about man disclosed in each is an abstraction and cannot represent the whole truth about man. The full truth, though never finally known in its fullness, can be approached only through a synthesis of these particular and partial truths.

A Christian teacher who holds some such view of the structure of knowledge may find his understanding of his own discipline affected in a number of ways. He may find it an effective approach to assessing the contribution of his own discipline and to recognizing its limitations. Hopefully such an assessment and recognition may be communicated to his students. The Christian teacher may also see more fully the values of other disciplines, at the same time being better prepared to resist their imperialism. He may be able to achieve a fine balance between the general or liberalizing aspects of his discipline and the specialized knowledge with which his subject matter deals. He may be more willing to help his students build bridges, to see interrelationships between his own and the other disciplines.

A peculiar problem arises for the Christian teacher, however, when he tries to come to terms with the issue of the relationship between religious knowledge or truth and other kinds of knowledge or truth, or to put it another way, when he faces the question of the relation of theology to the various liberal arts disciplines. Perhaps all knowledge does form one whole; perhaps all knowledge does refer to a real world constituted by God and his works. Perhaps all truth is then in some sense truth about God. If so, we may as Christians regard every discipline as a holy or religious study. Such a view does not settle the question as to whether there is another kind of privileged knowledge of God (revelation), nor does it answer the problem of the possible relationships between the two. We shall have to return to this problem later in this discussion, and again in succeeding chapters.

Both of these approaches for relating a given discipline to the Christian faith have their merits. I would like to suggest another. Though this third view has not been fully explored, it seems to me particularly worth while. Apart from any obvious attempts which a discipline may make to deal with the content of religious life or experience, apart from any serious effort to point to a possible synthesis of knowledge, there are latent or implicit theological issues in every one of the disciplines. These are the issues which need to be recognized and lifted up. The Christian teacher needs to be conscious of the implications of the subject matter he teaches for or against the Christian interpretation of life. I shall be illustrating this approach at greater length in the following chapters with reference to particular disciplines, but it may be valuable at this point to indicate in a more general way the meaning of the phrase "latent or implicit theological issues." To do this, I shall need to say something first about the nature of theology itself.

Theology deals with man's experience of values; it deals not so much with particular values, though this is part of its task, as with what is held to be the source of values. It is concerned with the multiplicity of goods which men seek and treasure, but its central theme has to do with what Calvin called the "fountain of all good." The focus of the theologian's study is upon that which sustains, nourishes, and creates the good in human life and experience. Religion is the *commitment* to that which sustains, nourishes, and creates the good in human life. Theology is the intellectual interpretation of that to which man commits himself.

To put the meaning of theology another way: the central theological problem is Job's problem. It is the problem of basic trust. The more experience each of us has of life, the more he realizes the insecurity of all human existence, the threat which hangs over every aspect of our lives. To be sure, there are things in our lives which are relatively dependable and trustworthy—family, friends, health, wealth, knowledge. Yet we know, if we look below the surface of our lives, that at any time we might, like Job, have all these things stripped away. What then? What can a man finally trust then? Seen in this light, religion is the trust; theology is the intellectual interpretation of that upon which we rest our trust.

Another way of stating the basic theological problem has been popularized by Paul Tillich. Tillich writes of the meaning of religion in terms of man's *ultimate concern*. God is man's ultimate concern; whatever concerns a man ultimately is his "god." There is no religion without ultimate concern, and the character and quality of a man's ultimate concern indicate the character and quality of his religion. "The object of theology is what concerns us ultimately. Only those propositions are theological which deal with their object in so far as it can become a matter of ultimate concern for us." [7]

Christian theology can be distinguished from other theologies because it represents a particular kind of interpretation of human existence regarding the source of values, or what is finally trustworthy, or what is of ultimate concern. Like all theology it is a human construct, the result of man's wrestling intellectually with the problem of how to understand that which he has found to sustain, nourish, and create the good in his life when he has committed himself to it. Particular theological interpretations are time and culture bound. They develop, change, are revised, abandoned, reconstructed, in response to changing patterns of thought and knowledge. So long, however, as men are found by God through Christ, so long as they find their own lives transformed and fulfilled in Christ, the Christian theologian has his task set for him. In a sense no one of us escapes the problem of theology, of thinking about our Christian faith. Not only is "mind" an inseparable part of man, but if there is language, there is thought. Language means thought, concepts, ideas. At the same time the Christian faith is not primarily thought; it is quite possible for a simple or unlearned individual to be a Christian without being a theologian in any technical or sophisticated sense. Yet I am convinced that though thinking about the Christian faith rises out of experience, it in turn molds and shapes the experience. It is important therefore for an individual to do the best thinking that he can about his faith. The more capable he is of thought, the more the demand is upon him to think carefully about his faith. Man's intellectual life cannot be separated from the rest of his life—in this case from his religious commitment. Every Christian intellectual, be he teacher, writer, or lawyer, has an obligation to bring the life of his mind into active and positive relationship to his ultimate concern, his basic trust, his commitment to what nourishes, sustains, and creates the good of his life. This means the attempt not only to interpret intellectually the trust, the concern, the commitment itself, but to relate so-called secular knowledge to this realm. Such an effort is important for the Christian teacher himself if he is to avoid split loyalties and compartmentalization in his own life. It is also important for the students whom he teaches. Many students find the Christian faith closed to them because of the time-bound character of the concepts and categories with which it is communicated. It is a scandal and an offense not because of its central meaning, for they never get to the central meaning, but because they are put off by modes of thought and expression which no longer communicate or which are irreconcilable with those of modern man. The Christian teacher owes it to himself, to his own integrity, to come to terms with this problem. If he would awaken in his students a sense of the meaningfulness of the Christian option, he owes it to his students to deal with it not only within his own discipline but also with reference to the realm of modern thought and knowledge as a whole.

To return to the meaning of the phrase "latent or implicit theological issues," it can now be said that such an issue exists in any discipline wherever that discipline can be related directly or indirectly to the problem of values and their source, to the problems of relative and final trust, or to the matter of ultimate concern. Perhaps I can illustrate this point by reference to the problem of truth. Few disciplines apart from theology and philosophy concern themselves in an explicit way with defining clearly the nature of truth. Yet each discipline, at least in the work of a specific scholar or group of scholars, presupposes a view of truth which may carry implicit claims far beyond the range of the particular discipline itself. Every methodology in every academic discipline hides or reveals assumptions as to the nature of truth. Sometimes there is no overt claim that a particular assumption about the nature of truth is to be universally accepted. Often, however, such a claim is covertly or unconsciously held. The Christian teacher needs to expose and examine such claims and their implications. For him and his students a whole series of questions will emerge. Is there one road to truth, or are there many? On what ground can they be justified? Does the ground for justification itself presuppose a prior assumption about the nature of truth? Are there different kinds of truth—an artistic, a scientific, a religious, an historical truth? If there are, how are they related to one another? Do they all have something to contribute to helping us understand and relate ourselves to what is ultimately trustworthy, what is worthy of our commitment and concern? Are there limits in principle to man's knowledge or to his appropriation of such knowledge or truth in an existential way? If so, what is their nature, and how do they affect inquiry in the various disciplines?

Even though a particular subject matter with which a given teacher is concerned may not include references either to religion or to the Christian faith, even though it may not be possible to see clearly how this segment of knowledge is related to a total synthesis which somehow is in the "mind of God," there still may be basic issues in a given discipline of great theological import. There may be implicit assumptions either which challenge the Christian theologian's interpretation of life or which support it. There may be insights and understandings which press for a re-examination and reconstruction of Christian theological formulations or which enlarge and sustain the Christian vision of life. There may be communicated information, ideas, and attitudes which hinder or help the transformation of the individual, the society, and the culture in the Christian image. All of these possibilities are important ones for the Christian teacher to explore. It is certainly not defensible to urge that each discipline should be taught as an adjunct either of theology or of the Christian faith, but it is arguable by the Christian that wherever in a given subject matter the student can be made aware of how man is to understand himself, nature, history, culture, or truth, that this effort should be made, since understanding in all of these areas may radically affect the way in which both the teacher and his students address the questions of ultimate trust, concern, or commitment. Such a position can be defended not only on the ground of the determinative significance of such issues within the discipline itself, but from the point of view of the meaning both of liberal education and of the Christian faith.

Perhaps the abiding issue, implicit in all the disciplines and already alluded to, has to do wth the relation of the knowledge or truth disclosed in and through the so-called secular disciplines and religious knowledge or truth. The relevant questions can be phrased in a variety of ways: How is the knowledge or truth with which the secular disciplines deal to be related to the knowledge or truth with which theology deals? How is knowledge or truth related to the Christian life itself? These are the old questions of the relation of faith and reason. The kind of assumption the Christian teacher makes here will very much affect his attitude toward his own discipline and the way in which he handles his subject matter. It will in part determine the way in which he sees the relationship between his Christian vocation and his specialized field of learning.

Newman again can take us part of the way in the exploration of this issue. One of the images he uses to describe the structure of knowledge is that of two great intersecting circles. The one circle contains knowledge gained from the study of the natural world; the other contains the knowledge gained through revelation of the supernatural world.

These two great circles of knowledge, as I have said, intersect; first, as far as supernatural knowledge includes truths and facts of the natural world, and secondly, as far as truths and facts of the natural world are on the other hand data for inferences about the supernatural. Still, allowing this interference to the full, it will be found, on the whole, that the two worlds and the two kinds of knowledge respectively are separated off from each other; and that, therefore, as being separate, they cannot on the whole contradict each other.[8]

Yet the conclusions of every science (including theology) are "revised and completed by each other,"[9] for all of them are abstractions.

I lay it down that all knowledge forms one whole, because its subject-matter is one; for the universe in its length and breadth is so intimately knit together, that we cannot separate off portion from portion, and operation from operation, except by a mental abstraction; and then again, as to its Creator, though He of course in His own Being is infinitely separate from it, and Theology has its departments towards which human knowledge has no relations, yet He has so implicated Himself with it, and taken it into His very bosom, by His presence in it, His providence over it, His impressions upon it, and His influences through it, that we cannot truly or fully contemplate it without in some main aspects contemplating Him.[10]

We can know something about God through his works. We can know something about God through revelation. Truth gained through reason and truth gained through revelation do not contradict each other. "Truth cannot contradict truth."

If anything seems to be proved by astronomer, or geologist, or chronologist, or antiquarian, or ethnologist, in contradiction to the dogmas of faith, that point will eventually turn out, first, *not* to be proved, or, secondly, not *contradictory,* or thirdly, not contradictory to any thing *really revealed,* but to something which has been confused with revelation.[11]

Another view is commonly put forward in our day by the Christian existentialists. They do not regard revelation as being a disclosure of truth in the sense of knowledge about God. Religious knowledge is personal, concerned, a matter of concrete encounter and relationship. In contrast, the ways of knowing in the various academic disciplines are objective, detached, by their very nature uncommitted. There may be objective knowledge of God through philosophy or metaphysics or even through biology or physics, but this is of no consequence to the religious life, for such a God is not God in the religious sense. He is an object, not a subject. He is not "Lord" of the individual's life. An objective relationship of "knowledge about" God destroys the relationship of an I to a Thou. It cuts the personal quality. It presupposes that the subject who knows transcends the object known. It removes the mystery and the depth. People who take this point of view regard secular learning or even theology grounded in human reason or general experience as irrelevant to the ultimate relationship of faith. Secular learning may be instrumental to the general pursuits of human life or even to the implementation of Christian responsibility in personal vocation and social endeavor, but it cannot contribute directly to the Christian's knowledge of God or give a directive to the Christian life.

There is much truth in this position taken by the existentialist. It is clear that there is a real distinction between the concrete relationship to God in trust, commitment, or ultimate concern and the intellectual understanding of this relationship in theology. It is clear also that there is an important distinction between theology which deals with the object of final trust, concern, and commitment and the other disciplines which deal with the relativities of human life and experience. Yet even if we admit these distinctions, the question is still unsettled. Can learning or knowledge in the various disciplines contribute, on the one hand, to man's understanding of the object of theology and religious faith and, on the other, help provide directives for the Christian life itself?

Perhaps objectivity and detachment if properly used may serve faith and the theological enterprise rather than destroy them. There may be a concerned objectivity and committed detachment which are both a phase of the theological task and a part of the life of faith. Truth seeking can be passionate and concerned. Doubt can be included within faith. Objectivity, detachment, doubt, can be regarded as the best protection man has against the distortions of his own sinfulness and the limitations of his finitude. Inquiry may be initiated in ultimate concern, move through a phase of objectivity, detachment, doubt, and issue in a fuller, more unified, more honest trust and commitment. Such a position would give to secular knowledge as well as to rational and empirical theological inquiry a constructive and positive end in relation to faith. The relationship between theology and secular learning would be that of a continuing dialogue. Both constructive and critical insights might come out of each of the perspectives as they are reciprocally related to one another.

Each Christian intellectual, each Christian scholar, has to come to terms with this problem. Whatever his decision, his attitude toward his own discipline will be affected. His understanding of the relationship of that discipline to his own faith and to the potential faith of his students will be altered. His attitude in turn will shape the way in which he handles his subject matter, the way he assesses its importance, the resources he finds in it for the Christian life and for the intellectual understanding of his faith. Taking "reason" as a symbol for secular inquiry and learning, he may, on the one hand, argue that the task of reason is to explore and comprehend its own limits. He may see in reason an apologetic tool. He may use it to comprehend the attacks which the modern world makes upon the Christian faith, whether these come from historical, sociological, psychological, or other studies. He may use it as a tool of defense. He may, on the other hand, use his secular learning as a means of communicating the faith and its implications to the surrounding secular culture and the secular mind, or as a means of reconciling the faith and new knowledge as such knowledge emerges on the human scene. Or finally, in addition, he may find in "reason" the critical and reconstructive resources for a more adequate intellectual interpretation of the faith, for the wedding of faith and reason in his own person and in the lives of his students.

Chapter III

THE CHRISTIAN TEACHER
AND THE HUMANITIES

THE ISSUES INTRODUCED IN THE PRECEDING DISCUSSION REQUIRE
sharper focusing. It is well and good to talk in general terms
of the Christian teacher's concern with his discipline, but
each of us will be ready with questions concerning the application of general principles to our specific teaching responsibilities. The task of providing a sharper focus through
directing attention to specific disciplines is delicate; no one
has much specialized knowledge outside his own field. The
man of letters, the social scientist, or the natural scientist
is likely to be theologically unsophisticated while the theologian may easily get beyond his own depth when he ad-
dresses the problems of literature, sociology, or biology.
We need more responsible and informed thinking about the
relation of the Christian faith to the liberal arts disciplines
among the teachers of every discipline, but until that day
the theologian concerned with higher education must take
his chances. He must venture opinions, judgments, and sug-
gestions with the hope that, however far of the mark he may
appear to go, what he has to say may at least provoke dis-

cussion within a field of study and that such discussion may lead to a more adequate statement of issues from within the field itself. This is the task I have laid upon myself. Rather than speak briefly of what may be possible within a large number of disciplines, I shall select one representative discipline from each of the major areas of study: the humanities, the social sciences, and the natural sciences.

Within the humanities many of us are most at home in literature. We have at least been exposed to poetry, drama, and the novel in our schooldays, and most of us have continued to read them as time allows. Imaginative literature, then, may well provide the most accessible illustrations of ways in which the Christian teacher of the humanistic disciplines may relate his faith to his discipline. The teaching of literature in American colleges and universities may have many objectives, but whatever its more distant goals it must be immediately directed toward the understanding and appreciation of the particular works chosen for study and toward the development of a discriminating judgment in the whole range of imaginative writing which the student may confront now and in later life. In so far as religious matters are relevant to the development of such understanding, appreciation, and discrimination, they may be legitimately brought into the program of study. The neglect of such matters not only communicates indifference to religious concern or a negative evaluation of it but also fosters the kind of religious ignorance which makes the intelligent facing of religious issues in the student's own life all but impossible. The Christian teacher is likely to be more sensitive at these points and knowing what is at stake, he ought to make a more direct effort to face the issues. He will not lug in religion where it is peripheral or irrelevant, but he is more likely to be able to see that in the deepest sense it is seldom peripheral to an understanding of the great works of the human mind.

I have already suggested that one of the legitimate and indeed necessary points at which the Christian teacher of literature must consider religious issues comes in the study of those works which have obviously been shaped by the personal religious convictions of the author or the religious spirit and culture of an age. The language and thought of religion, religious feeling, theological ideas, have given content and molded the form of much Western literature. The vocabulary, the allusions, the imagery and style, of many writers can be understood only by grasping the religious dimension of the context out of which they wrote.

A powerful illustration of this is the work of Dante. In the *Divine Comedy* it is not simply that the vocabulary, the allusions, and the imagery are incomprehensible apart from a knowledge of scripture and tradition, but a grasp of the very structure of the work demands a knowledge of the Christian faith. Dante himself, as Dorothy Sayers has so clearly shown, would have his readers understand his poem at four levels.[1] The *Divine Comedy* has a literal meaning: namely, the state of souls after death. Understanding at this level means acquaintance with traditional Christian teachings about heaven and hell. This literal meaning then itself is to be understood symbolically and concurrently at three other levels. The first, which Dante calls the allegorical, signifies the life of man in its social and historical dimensions. The second, the moral, reveals the passage of the individual Christian from a state of sin to a state of grace. The third, the anagogical, or mystical, refers to the Way of Contemplation, the way by which the mystic is accorded the

Beatific Vision. No one of these interpretations of the *Divine Comedy* can be understood without a knowledge of the context of religious ideas out of which they issue: the Christian view of man, the world, and God.

The Christian teacher has not done his job if he is satisfied merely with helping the student gain the information necessary to understanding the ideas a writer expresses. Nor has he done his job if he is satisfied to approach a poem or play or novel solely as a self-contained work of art. Whatever we may finally conclude about "art for art's sake" and the relation of imaginative literature to knowledge, the fact of the matter is as Middleton Murry says: "Great poets mean what they say." [2] It is part of the task of the Christian teacher to help the student enter into the thought world and the feeling world of the writer, to confront what he has to say, to be sensitive enough to his world of feeling, that he faces the meaning of that work "existentially." Teaching of this kind moves beyond objective acquaintance to yea and nay, to confirmation or rejection, to appropriation and participation. It becomes a means of true education. In the case of Dante it is not enough to be sophisticated theologically so that one understands what the church has traditionally taught about life after death. One must see the issues which are at stake for one's own life beneath the theological trappings of another age and the outmoded metaphysic of another day. One must go further and confront what Dante is saying about the inner life of man, about his own inner life, about yours and mine. This is the story of a conversion, of a turning from one way toward another. In every great work of literature the reader is confronted with an either/or, but such confrontation demands that students and teachers alike penetrate below the surface. As Dorothy Sayers says so well:

> The thing that the modern reader and critic find so difficult, when confronted by a great poet, is to accept him. To realize what he is saying, to believe that he means what he says, to admit that what he says matters—all this is disquieting. It is more comfortable to explain him away, with his meaning and his greatness and his power. Despite all our surface liking for toughness and violence, ours is a timid generation, wincing at decision and envious of other men's conclusions.[3]

What is obvious in the case of ostensibly religious poetry like that of Dante, Milton, or the later Eliot is of equal concern in the work of many other writers. A Wordsworth, a Keats, or a Byron does not escape the climate of contending religious and philosophical ideas. They do not transcend their personal religious experience even though much of their poetry may seem to be "secular" in nature. It may not be desirable or necessary to scrutinize them against such strict canons of Christian orthodoxy as does a historian of ideas like Professor Hoxie Fairchild, but the same demand for understanding, appreciation, and confrontation requires a penetration of the ideology and sensibilities of their time and place, inclusive of religious thought and feeling.

Less obvious is the discrimination demanded of students and teachers in the study of writers who seem clearly detached from the religious heritage. For T. S. Eliot to discern a "dim recognition of the direction of beatitude" in Baudelaire's concern with the real problem of good and evil and in his perception that what really matters is sin and redemption demands a fine sense of what the Christian faith is all about.[4] Or for a student to see in the apparent rebellion of many contemporary writers against traditional Christian modes of thought a "necessary criticism, correction and protest" which is itself rooted in our religious tradition, the teacher must do a great deal to acquaint his class with the meaning of the prophetic spirit within the Christian faith.[5] Amos Wilder suggests that the custody of the Christian heritage has today passed over to a considerable degree at least into the "keeping of secularized groups and forces." He believes that the spirit may be speaking to the churches not only through the laity but through the disaffected, and even through the apostates and the Gentiles.[6] If this is true, it is an important conclusion, and yet one can hardly assess its merits without a fundamental grasp of the essentials of the Christian faith.

I have been maintaining that the Christian teacher of literature will give full attention to the part religious thought and feeling play in works studied by his students; he will do so in the interest of a more adequate understanding of the works themselves. He will also recognize that giving time to these matters both calls attention to the significant place of religious concerns in man's life and provides his students with some of the materials by means of which intelligent discussion and decision in the area of religion may be made. Understanding and appreciation, whether at the level of objective knowledge or at the deeper level of sensibility (which includes such knowledge), do not exhaust the possibilities for the Christian teacher of literature. Beyond understanding and appreciation of literature there is the task of criticism, evaluation, discriminating judgment. One might even hope that courses in the history of literature might be taught in such a fashion that

19170

at least some valid principles of discrimination become a part of the accumulated learning of each of the students.

Education ought to ensure the recognition of excellence. The teacher of literature can help his students develop such sensitivity in regard both to the formal side of artistic expression and to the feeling and thought which are expressed. The latter is peculiarly important for the average reader. Valuable as it may be for all of us to continue to read the great works, the classics, or even the respectable writers of our own time, much of our reading will not be of that kind. Many read for pleasure more than edification. They read for amusement or purely for pleasure and relaxation. It may be that this kind of reading in the long run has the most formative influence on the public mind and on the individual's life and spirit. I am inclined to agree with Eliot when he suggests that it is just this kind of literature which may have the "greatest and least suspected influence upon us." [7] Such literature, which we read with the least effort, is likely to have the easiest and most insidious influence upon us. It is contemporary literature—the popular novelists and the popular plays—which needs to be read with sharp critical tools. The solution is not to exile the poets or censor writers but to develop the capacities of discrimination and critical judgment among the readers of today and tomorrow.

Certain of the most influential of the contemporary schools of literary criticism have been castigated for centering their attention on formal and technical problems.[8] They have been accused of preoccupation with technique, with the poem, the novel, or the play solely as an aesthetic object, seeking to escape from the problems of belief, knowledge, truth, external reference. Whatever the merits of this criticism of the critics, and a layman's reading of men like Tate, Eliot, does not fully support it, it seems likely that the critic as Christian, or the teacher of literature as Christian teacher, could hardly limit himself to such preoccupations. Certainly the Christian teacher of literature will be concerned with technical aesthetic criticism, and this concern may itself be related to theological convictions, but he will, I think, want to subject a writer's art to a different kind of scrutiny as well, and this too in the name of criticism, discrimination, excellence. I have already pointed to the way in which it is legitimate for the Christian teacher to bring into his discussion the formal religious influences, cultural or personal, whch are necessary to the understanding of a work. Some authors intend to communicate a religious message. What I mean to suggest now is that the Christian teacher of literature needs to look more deeply at the works he and his students are to study, to discover, whatever may be the conscious intention of the authors, the actual pattern of belief expressed in and through the works of art. As my colleague Nathan Scott has so ably pointed out, the issues of religion are never merely peripheral in literature.[9] There is implicit, if not explicit, in every work of art a vision of life and of man which that work expresses. A writer's beliefs may not be propositional in nature, and certainly to translate them too simply into propositions whose validity is to be assessed in the same fashion that a scientist's might be may be unjust. But this implicit vision, this giving shape and significance to the primary data of experience, is a part of the work of art and, while not finally separable from form and structure, nevertheless carries a referential relationship beyond the work itself.[10] This vision too must be assessed, evaluated, subjected to criticism. Such criticism might be made from a variety of perspectives by critics possessed of differing religious loyalties or philosophical commitments, though many students of literature decline to make any such judgments. The Christian teacher, however, must undertake criticism of this kind, and he will subject these patterns of belief to a theological criticism, a criticism from the perspective of the Christian faith. For the Christian at least, literary criticism cannot be simply the criticism or evaluation of the aesthetic form of a work, of the quality of its mode of expression. Criticism must cut deeper into the matter of the validity of the view of life which is expressed and communicated. It need not necessarily imply a negative judgment, but it would mean the exposure of the basic issues. It may mean understanding the work in relation to the conflicting views of man and the world present both in history and on the contemporary scene. It means helping students become aware of what is at stake in the vision of life which informs the poet, the playwright, or the novelist.[11]

In all of this I am not talking about what is sometimes called didactic writing, and certainly not about what the French call "la piece a these." Imaginative literature is not simply the "rhetorical garb for truthful propositions which are to be derived from science or philosophy."[12] And yet writers are saying something which communicates a way of looking at experience, feeling significance, understanding man, which may be more *or* less translatable into other forms of statement. It is not always necessary that a writer should be fully conscious of the implications of what he is saying; some authors seem less conscious of this level of meaning in their work than others. Nor is it necessary to maintain that every writer is a thinker, though I would very much demur from Eliot's view that men like Shakespeare and Dante were not thinkers, since that "was not their job." [13] Some writers are more "thinkers" than are others, but even in the case of a great thinker the form and structure of his imaginative creation is not simply rhetorical garb. That a view of life is to be found in great imaginative literature is not an illusion (Eliot). Whether we call the view of life knowledge as does Allen Tate when he writes: "Literature is the complete knowledge of man's experience, and by knowledge I mean that unique and formed intelligence of the world of which man alone is capable," [14] or whether, reserving the word "knowledge," we speak of literature as "giving us an experiential grasp of our world which eludes the systematized abstractions of the knowledge-giving disciplines," [15] we are pointing to the fact that imaginative literature does say something about what is important to man. It is this element in literature which Eliot himself was calling attention to in his remarks about the effects of popular literature, insidious or otherwise, on our moral and religious existence. It is this element which the Christian teacher needs to help his students evaluate and criticize.

What I have called theological criticism, the clarification and elucidation of the vision of life and man, implicit in works of imaginative literature, together with a discriminating judgment of its adequacy, is closely related to the theologian's technical task within his own discipline. In much of his work the theologian deals with myth, legend, the imaginative interpretation of concrete, historical, and personal events. The language of imaginative literature is not utterly different from the language of myth or other forms of religious discourse. The theologian must be their interpreter and critic. He may or may not try to translate such meanings into verifiable propositions. His own language may vary in its closeness or its distance from that of the sciences. What the theologian must do as interpreter and critic of the expressions of personal or communal religious experience, the Christian critic of literature must do for imaginative literature.

The underlying attitudes of the author are disclosed not only in the direct statement of ideology but in style, vocabulary, description, and characterization. What he selects, what interests him, the images he uses, all reveal something of his experience of life, his values, what he thinks is important. The descriptions an engineer, a botanist, a city dweller, might give of the countryside might differ very greatly from one another and from that of a farmer. A vivid illustration of the difference in the way two authors describe an experience, feel its significance, reflect on its meaning, will be seen by comparing the famous chapter in Jean-Paul Sartre's novel *Nausea* in which Roquentin, the hero, sits in a public garden, staring at the root of a chestnut tree, and that chapter in Herman Melville's *Omoo* in which the author describes the Polynesian coco palm. These two chapters ought to be read in their entirety one after the other both to get the general contrast in feeling and to see the difference in the selection of words, the allusions. I can reproduce only a small impression of this contrast here.

In Sartre's chapter Roquentin is in the park; he drops down on a bench "between great black tree-trunks, between the black, knotty hands reaching towards the sky. A tree scrapes at the earth under my feet with a black nail." [16] He is overcome by the absurdity of the root before him and the "flaunting abundance" of what he sees before him. This particular root

existed in such a way that I could not explain it. Knotty, inert, nameless, it fascinated me, filled my eyes, brought me back unceasingly to its own existence. In vain to repeat: "This is a root" —it didn't work any more. I saw clearly that you could not pass from its function as a root, as a breathing pump, *to that,* to this hard and compact skin of a sea lion, to this oily, callous, headstrong look. The function explained nothing: it allowed you to understand generally that it was a root, but not *that one* at all. This root, with its colour, shape, its congealed movement, was . . . below all explanation.

Roquentin sees the blackness of the root.

It *looked* like a colour, but also . . . like a bruise or a secretion, like an oozing—and something else, an odour, for example, it melted into the odour of wet earth, warm, moist wood, into a black odour that spread like varnish over this sensitive wood, in a flavour of chewed, sweet fibre.

The "flaunting abundance," the profusion of beings without origin, the impression of the excess of existence, overcame him as a presence:

It was there, in the garden, toppled down into the trees, all soft, sticky, soiling everything, all thick, a jelly. And I was inside, I with the garden. I was frightened, furious, I thought it was so stupid, so out of place, I hated this ignoble mess. Mounting up, mounting up as high as the sky, spilling over, filling everything with its gelatinous slither, and I could see depths upon depths of it reaching far beyond the limits of the garden . . . as far as the eye could reach.

Compare this picture of abundance, represented as absurdity, as nauseating, as a symbol of the contingency and absurdity of Roquentin's own existence with Melville's picture of the coco palm. To the Polynesian this tree is the Tree of Life. It provides him with food, clothing, shelter, medicine, weapons, even oil to embalm his dead. In older days it was the symbol of regal authority. It is prodigal in its fruitfulness. Its aspect is imposing. "Asserting its supremacy by an erect and lofty bearing, it may be said to compare with other trees as man with inferior creatures." Melville seems to share the natives' regard for the tree, for he writes of a grove of these trees:

> At noonday, this grove is one of the most beautiful, serene, witching places that ever was seen. High overhead, are ranges of green rustling arches; through which the sun's rays come down to you in sparkles. You seem to be wandering through illimitable halls of pillars; everywhere you catch glimpses of stately aisles, intersecting each other at all points. A strange silence, too, reigns, far and near; the air flushed with the mellow stillness of a sunset.[17]

What is true of distinguished writers like that of Sartre or Melville is equally true of literary trash. A brilliant analysis of one example of the latter was made a few years ago by Christopher LaFarge in his *Saturday Review* article "Mickey Spillane and His Bloody Hammer." The accounts of the exploits of Mike Hammer, Spillane's vigilante-killer, depict clearly a way of thinking and feeling about life. Spillane's is a picture of sadism made into a way of life, a sadism which is held up "as a justifiable means to an admirable end."[18]

Theodore Spencer's Lowell Lectures, *Shakespeare and the Nature of Man,* analyzes a very different view of life found in total corpus of Shakespeare's works. Again, however, description and analysis are only the first step. Standards of judgment must be brought to bear on what is revealed. This is the task of a Christian critic, and the Christian teacher of literature, while withholding dogmatic pronouncements, may certainly make his own standards clearly understood and should be obligated to help students understand what issues are at stake.

Such study of literary works is more personal, more existential, than an effort which stops at objective understanding. It may also be more controversial, but if students are allowed to respond freely and honestly, the educational impact of such considerations are likely to be of great value. The student and the teacher may both be goaded into self-examination. They will have to raise questions as to the truth or validity of the various visions of man and of life. They may be forced to face the problem of the meaning of life through such personal encounter with the conflicting affirmations and negations of the writer's world view, even though world view in this respect may not be something that can be fully encapsulated in propositions which are in the literal sense true or false.

What I have been calling theological criticism—the clarification, analysis, and evaluation of the vision of life and man implicit in a work—may be carried a step further in closer relationship to literary criticism of the narrower and more formal kind. It seems clear that the formal *structure* of a literary work may also subtly reflect and mediate a world view. If this is true, it might even be possible to produce a Christian poetics, a distinctively Christian theory of literature. As Aristotle's *Poetics* reflect a Greek view of the world and man, so a Christian theory of literature would reflect the Christian interpretation of human experience. As the relationships among the various elements within the structure of a Greek tragedy illustrate Aristotle's theory of dramatic movement, the relationships among the various elements in a Christian play or novel would illustrate the Christian theory of literature. I am not sure how far such a thesis can be carried. It is true, however, that a different kind of dramatic movement takes place when human experience is understood as a story of human freedom, guilt, sin, and redemption rather than as a story of fate and doom. The formal elements of character, plot, thought, and so on, will be present in both, but the detailed depiction of character and the unraveling of plot will differ greatly. One of my colleagues, Preston Roberts, has written about this problem.[19] He has proposed the construction of a Christian theory of dramatic tragedy, distinguishing it from both the Greek view of tragedy and the modern skeptical view. According to Roberts a Christian tragedy can be only a tragedy of freedom. A Greek tragedy is a tragedy of fate. The flaw in the Greek tragic hero involves erring judgment; in the Christian tragic hero it involves guilt and sin. Greek tragedy moves from "ignorance to the bitterness of knowledge"; the Christian, "from sin to judgment and forgiveness." Greek tragedy interprets the human situation as beyond redemption; in the Christian view the tragedy of the human situation is not denied, but it is seen as redeemable. Seen in these terms the "plays of Shakespeare and the novels of Dostoevski are in a profound sense Christian dramatic tragedies." It is the difference among the "violence and despair of Prometheus' 'I am wronged,'" the "vision of Oedipus standing fixed, sightless, and maimed," and the movement beyond tragedy reflected in the shift from "Lear's 'what cause in nature makes these hard hearts?' to Edgar's, 'Ripeness is all!' " [20]

Recognition of these subtler influences of theological motif and world view as they affect the actual structure of a literary work may be an important part of the teacher's task. Understanding, appreciation, and evaluation are the primary goals, but a movement in the direction of these goals may bring the student face to face with the problem of his own interpretation of life. It may confront him with the necessity of determining for himself what interpretation of the human situation comes closest to representing the complexity and the meaning of life as he himself has known it, vicariously through the work of art and directly through his own experience.

So far we have been concerned with the theological issues implicit in literary works themselves. Few students of literature have been satisfied to limit themselves to the poem, the novel, or the play as isolated objects. They have also directed attention to the creative process by which imaginative literature comes into being and the effect of the work on its audience. Perhaps teachers of literature have given least classroom time to discussions of the creative process, and yet here is a mystery which is rich with implication for the Christian. The literary artist is a creator. At least he is creative in bringing new meanings, new richness of value, into human experience. How is this to be understood? Is the emergence of new meaning and value an accident? Is it simply to be described as being within human intent and control? What is the nature of the creative act? What supports and promotes it? What makes it possible? What thwarts it? What are the criteria by which it is to be evaluated or judged? I think questions like these are worth the teacher's attention and the student's interest.

A class might well read selections from Brewster Ghiselin's symposium *The Creative Process* to see how the writers themselves describe and understand the processes out of which creation comes. It is important to understand the psychological dimension of such experience, but it is equally important to assess its larger significance. May we say with Berdyaev that the creative activity of the writer, the artist, or the ordinary man points to "another world," or better, to a deeper dimension of the objectified world we know in ordinary experience? Does it not only symbolize the world of spirit but also hold within itself the power of awakening spirit? Can we see in such creativeness a means of healing, a way of overcoming evil? May not the achievement of beauty in the creative act, in every creative reception of the creative act, be both the key to ultimate meaning and a revelation of the divine?

To see in the creativeness of the writer something which touches on that deeper dimension of reality which one might call spirit, to see in the achievements of creativity the symbolization of spirit and the power of awakening spirit, is to come close to the view which Paul Tillich presents in his analysis of modern art. What Tillich says about art might appropriately be said of literature too. Starting from the premise that God is present in secular existence as much as he is present in the sacred, he points out that a picture may express or fail to express religious meaning in a variety of ways. A work of art may have a nonreligious style and a nonreligious content, it may have religious style and a nonreligious content, it may have a nonreligious style and a religious content, or it may have a religious style and a religious content. None of these characteristics is determinative so far as the religious meaning of the work of art is concerned. One needs always to ask: "What does this picture express in terms of an ultimate interpretation of human existence?" [21] What does it say about ultimate concern? A picture without religious style or content may yet show forth the "power of being," not directly but indirectly. Embodied in a variety of forms, communicated through a variety of contents, the "power of being" may itself be "present" for the sensitive person in a play, a novel, a poem, a piece of sculpture, or a work of music. Or a work may fail to communicate the power of being. It may incarnate no ultimate concern. It may speak neither out of nor to the human situation. This it may fail to do even though it is permeated by religious style and filled with ostensibly religious content. "Power of being" for Tillich means the presence of that upon which everything depends, of the ground of being, or of God in every particular aspect or structure of being.[22] To say that man may sense the "power of being" through a work of art or literature is to say that that work has a revealing power. It reveals something of the depth and mystery of what concerns us ultimately, of that upon which all of us depend for both existence and meaning. That which is the ground of our being, which determines our being or our not being, expresses itself and may reveal itself in and through the structures of particular beings.

The ultimate meaning of the creative act then is to be understood not solely in relation to an autonomous product, but in relation to the deeper dimension of reality out of which it emerges and beyond this in relation to its capacity to reveal through the particular structures of being the power of being itself, the depth and mystery of that upon which all of us depend for existence and meaning. For this reason the response of the reader, the listener, the audience, has an important place in the Christian critic's assessment of a work. An important part of the theological significance of a work is seen when we ask the questions: What in fact does this work do to its reader? What is communicated? What is the human response, and what explains its character? Does a work of literature do more than confront its readers with the basic questions of human existence, with some ultimate interpretation of the human situation? Does it go further and contribute something toward the positive shaping of new attitudes and responses, toward the making of personal being? Is it religious in the sense that it transforms character, "cleanses the inward parts" in so far as this "depends on the man himself and on what is permanent in the nature of things"? Is it religious in the sense that it contributes to the emergence of what A. N. Whitehead calls "individual worth of character"? [23]

Some clarification of what these questions might mean concretely can be given by citing Walter Horton's account of what he calls "one of the most impressive religious experiences I have ever had." Horton writes:

One of the most impressive religious experiences I have ever had came to me, not in church, but—shades of my Puritan ancestors, avert your faces!—in a New York theater, where John Drinkwater's *Abraham Lincoln* was then playing. As scene succeeded scene, and the soul of Lincoln was more and more completely revealed—triumphing over his own misgivings, forsaking ease for the sake of the well-being of all, unflinching in his opposition to evil, but overcoming evil with compassion, giving his life at length as a ransom for many—I found myself at last looking upon the stage with the eyes of a worshiper. . . . Consciously or unconsciously, each person there worshiped God that evening. I felt it in the applause, and in the still more significant silences; and the fellowship of adoration added greatly to the depth of it for all of us; for it helped us to feel that this was not merely *my* God but *our* God,—yes, the God of all mankind.

Horton continues, analyzing this experience:

Now what do I mean by saying I met God in Drinkwater's *Lincoln?* Well, what did I mean at the time? Let me scrutinize the workings of my mind. I think that Lincoln's divineness in my eyes consisted precisely in that "combination of ideality and final efficacity" which was the criterion of the divine for William James. I got a double impression of moral nobility in the highest degree, and of irresistible power. In the first place, Lincoln humbled me as the ideal always humbles the actual; his human figure, with its homely qualities and obvious limitations, became, as it were, translucent, and through it shone a pure and unwavering light, the light of the ideal, making me long unutterably to be like him—and unlike myself. But this was not all; he was for me the incarnation of irresistible might. This was, if possible, the stronger of the two impressions. "This is the spirit that is bound to win," I said to myself. I saw it triumphing before my eyes—winning the respect of the supercilious Seward and the cantankerous Stanton, turning a condemned youth into a hero and bidding fair to bind a nation into a unity based on justice and mutual forgiveness. I saw it hushing a miscellaneous New York audience into reverence. And then, the theater could not contain it. I looked out beyond the stage into the tangled world, and I saw that spirit, embodied in the messages of President Wilson, putting an end to a great war, and arousing fabulous hopes in the hearts of all the peoples—and chaos and despair rushing back upon the scene when that spirit which had governed us in war failed to get incorporated in the treaty of peace. I thought of the triumphs of many folks, ordinary

63

and extraordinary, missionaries, reformers, plain people, in whom this spirit finds more or less imperfect embodiment, and I said to myself: "It's irresistible; its almighty. No one can stop it. Nail it to a cross and it smiles at you and continues. Sooner or later, it is going to capture the last redoubt, and rule in the hearts of *all*."

If my enthusiasm had permitted me to stop at this point, I should simply have been affirming, as you see, that the God whom I glimpsed in Lincoln was *a tendency in human history, a growing social entity,* if you will, of such a nature that it was bound to overcome all obstacles and become the organizing principle of human society and the object of each human individual's allegiance. Poetizing a bit, I should easily have arrived at the conception of an Invisible King or Captain of mankind, growing with the growth of mankind, yet always leading on. . . .

But I did not stop at this point, just on the margin of metaphysics, where all good humanists draw the line. I pressed on—rashly, perhaps—and it began to rain metaphysics, thick and fast. "The spirit of Lincoln," I said in my haste, "*must* triumph. The nature of things is such—*human* nature, of course, but nature in general too. The universe is built that way; that's why the universe is on his side." "Yes,"—and here I took a terrific leap, from an impersonal moral order to an anthropomorphic deity—"there is at the heart of things a spirit like that of Lincoln, a personality like his." Thus did the primitive Christian reason concernng Christ; and thus, I admit it, I reasoned concerning Lincoln.[24]

My purpose in citing this long quotation from Walter Horton is to maintain neither that a literary work should stimulate theological reflection nor that it should deliberately aim at moral improvement, as it is sometimes called. Rather it is to point to the fact that literature may have revelatory power and that it may be the vehicle, the channel, or the catalyst through which the illumination and transformation of personal life take place. That this is so is of theological significance. That this is so is of concern to the student and critic of literature. Illumination and transformation may not be the specific goal of the writer, but he may have so succeeded in presenting us with the organization of the primary subject matter of experience, so introduced us to the *fullness* of experience, that illumination and transformation are almost inescapable. This, I take it, is the specific intention of some writers. Gabriel Marcel, the French playwright and philosopher, writes of his own work:

> The chief function of the theatre [is] not to relate the particular to the general or to a law or to an idea, but to awaken or re-awaken in us the consciousness of the infinite which is concealed in the particular. To my mind, in this way alone can the dramatist penetrate to our centre and arrive at that zone of concrete universality which music and metaphysics reach by other convergent ways.[25]

The aim is "to transfigure our interior landscape and illuminate it in a flash with a light which seems to come from beyond." [26]

Speaking of Marcel's success in this venture, Rosalind Heywood has written:

> His great gift is to startle us into a new awareness, and also into a new honesty *vis-a-vis* ourselves. For relentlessly though gently, those selves are laid bare, the selves, moreover, which we have so far succeeded in concealing even from ourselves.[27]

Those who have read Marcel's plays, like *Ariadne, A Man of God,* or *The Funeral Pyre,* can bear witness to his capacity so to involve his readers in the thoughts and feelings of his characters that they do find their own "interior landscape" illuminated and transfigured.

Chapter IV

THE CHRISTIAN TEACHER
AND THE SOCIAL SCIENCES

I HAVE TRIED TO SKETCH SOME OF THE IMPORTANT POINTS AT which one can talk about the theological issues in literature and so by implication in the other humanistic disciplines as well, though each particular discipline will have its own unique possibilities. It is difficult to know which of the social sciences to select for illustrative purposes. Many of the issues implicit in one are relevant to the others. History, sociology, anthropology, and psychology each make a claim upon the student who would understand his own situation and his own life. All of them have something important to say about the nature of religion itself and about the Christian religion in particular. One can study the history of religions and the history of a particular religion. One can study social phenomena within religious communities and the part religion plays in the relationship between and within social groups. One can study religious aspects of a culture or the part religion plays in the life of the individual. Just as in the case of the study of the religious backgrounds of a literary work or an age or in the study of the religious outlook and experience of an author, the illumination of such matters will undoubtedly raise theological issues for some. It is difficult to remain uninvolved, to see no connections between the problems raised by the religious commitments of another society, culture, or individual and the problems found in one's own society, culture, or personal life. It is difficult to study the history of some other period, group, or individual without raising questions about the meaning which may lie hidden there for oneself or one's own historical period.

In the social sciences as in the study of literature, however, there are other levels at which theological issues arise. While these issues are disclosed in any of the social sciences, they are especially evident within the various psychological disciplines. They are seen with particular clarity when one considers the problem of methodology and the possibility of the normative character of these disciplines. Since a discussion of this latter issue will illuminate many of the methodological questions it is perhaps better to deal with it first.

After reading a good deal in current psychological discussion, I have become convinced as a layman that much of it is normative in character. Even many of the psychologists who defend the strictly scientific nature of their discipline, and hence its nonvaluational character, produce work which contains hidden and sometimes openly affirmed normative assumptions and conclusions. To say that their thinking is often implicitly normative is to say that they treat values in a regulative, not simply in a descriptive, fashion. This does not mean that all psychological thinking is of this kind. In so far, however, as the various segments of psychological study are drawn together into an interpretation of man in his wholeness, the normative character of much psychological writing becomes apparent. Some psychologists will deny this; some will affirm it. One of the theological issues implicit in the discipline itself is a forthright facing of this question on its own account. Once one admits the possibility of a positive answer to such a question, the further problem must be met as to the source and nature of the norms which are relevant to the psychological disciplines. Are they simply derived from the larger cultural norms and to be accepted as such? Are they to be subjected to philosophical or theological scrutiny and defense? Or can they possibly be derived empirically from within the discipline itself? If the latter is the case, what is the relation of such norms to those which are culturally carried or philosophically and theologically derived?

These questions are highly abstract. Their meaning may become clearer by concrete illustration and nowhere clearer perhaps than in the areas of clinical psychology, psychiatry, and psychoanalysis. Each of these disciplines not only helps to clarify man's understanding of himself and so raises theological issues, but each of them implies normative presuppositions. Difficult as the problem may be to deal with, each of these disciplines contains within itself clear or vague ideas, criticized or uncriticized notions, having to do with "normality," "maturity," "mental health," "adjustment," the goals of therapy. These are normative notions. The clinical psychologist, the psychiatrist, the psychoanalyst, have some kind of operating perspective in terms of which they diagnose that something is "wrong" with the individual with whom they are working; they have some kind of working criteria by which to evaluate progress; they have some kind of guiding principle by which they judge when analysis should be terminated, when a client is to be dismissed, when a mental hospital patient can be released. Further than this they probably have implicit in all their thinking some kind of picture of what a "fully functioning individual" would be like, of what a "real person" would be, of what characteristics "self-actualizing people" in fact possess. Whence come such notions? How valid are they? By what criteria and from what perspective are they to be examined? How do they compare with normative propositions derived theologically or philosophically? Are they in conflict, or do they support one another? On what ground and within what context could tentative or final decisions be made?

Lest it be assumed that such normative questions arise only for these branches of psychology which are directed toward practical responsibilities, I would quickly add that they only appear more clearly there. They are in fact present in any of the psychological disciplines which deal with man in his wholeness. They may also appear in some of the segmental approaches to man's life and experience. Let me illustrate, using the work of one of the ablest and best-known personality psychologists.

Gordon W. Allport is a psychologist who is interested in understanding the total person. As psychologist he would clearly distinguish between psychology and ethics. "The psychology of personality must be kept free from confusion with the problems of evaluation," he writes.[1] "No psychologist *qua* psychologist," for example, "can tell how a child ought to be brought up. The most he can do is to disclose human nature as it is, and then, *after a moral code has been chosen,* find out means of incentive and training that will achieve the end desired."[2] Any guidance a psychologist may offer is not psychology at all; "it is pure ethics, springing from an uncritical acceptance of the normative ideal of 'perfect adjustment.' " [3] Allport's view of the nonnormative character of psychology as a social science is clear and uncompromising. Yet Allport himself in what some might call his most valuable chapters in his classic study of personality outlines a theory of maturity centering in three major criteria: extension of self, self-objectification, and a unifying philosophy of life. These are "general criteria" by which to distinguish a "fully developed personality from one that is still unripe"; they are "universal and indispensable." [4] To most of us such a characterization would seem to be normative. We would prefer to be "fully developed" rather than "still unripe." We might still recognize that there are a great variety of ways in which we can extend our selfhood and objectify ourselves. There are a great number of unifying philosophies of life which might serve us equally well. The status of such criteria is not completely clear in Allport's own thought. Are they ethical norms imported self-consciously into psychology, or are they descriptions based upon observation of the full flowering of human personality? There is some evidence that Allport regards them as derived from within the discipline itself. He writes: "In this doctrine of traits no psychological disposition in and of itself is intrinsically desirable or undesirable." [5] One trait may not be always good and another always bad, yet, even for Allport, the trait of self-deception presents a "weak case." "If any trait of personality is intrinsically desirable, it is the disposition and ability to see oneself in perspective." [6] Whether this is a psychological judgment on Allport's part or a philosophical one is hard to say. It is clear that a psychological defense could be made of it. Why, for example, would self-objectification (as over against self-deception) be a good even in psychological terms? The answer might be given that unless we accept the *status quo* as the final good for any individual, self-understanding is the only key to consciously guided change. The one developmental "trait" which makes possible ongoing development, the one value which makes possible the increase of values, is that of self-understanding. Some normative notion like that of "growth" seems clearly implied. One might argue then from within the discipline itself that certain kinds, types, or structures of personality are "good" because they and they alone contain the possibility or more possibilities for the increase of value for that personality. Other kinds of personality organization are "bad" since they cut off or thwart the increase of value for the individual.

Questions of this kind can be duplicated in the other social sciences. Are there transcultural norms or trans-societal norms which, arising out of social and cultural studies, prescribe, even if in a vague and general way, the criteria for a good society or a good culture? Or are there no such norms available from any source? Or is their source philosophy or theology alone? Such issues having to do with the normative character of inquiry in the social sciences, however we deal with them, illustrate the explicit nature of the possible relationship to the Christian faith and to theology contained in these disciplines. Theology deals with values, with what sustains and increases values. These disciplines themselves either deal with values, play a critical role in relation to values derived from other perspectives, or may be instrumental to the implementation of value commitments emerging from other human concerns. In any one and in all of these cases the Christian faith has a stake in the social sciences, and Christian theology can both learn from and contribute to their ongoing discussion.

Apart from value questions of this kind and the contributions which the social sciences may make to an understanding of man and his life, the principal context within which theological issues arise has to do with methodology. What must be said here is close to what must be said in the natural sciences. Indeed some psychologists like to think of their discipline as a natural science, and their aim is to study psychological data using the methods of the natural scientist. In any discipline the methods used, if study is to be productive of new understanding, must be relevant to the problems to be investigated. Among many teachers and a good many investigators self-consciousness about method, about the implications and presuppositions of particular methods, is not very great. When the teacher is unsophisticated in handling the problem of method, it is likely that his students will be too. The hidden presuppositions implicit in a given method, the basic philosophical outlook of an investigator as determining procedure and the interpretation of results, the critical examination of the limits of particular methods, are infrequently the subject matter of reading or class discussion. This is understandable in much elementary and introductory work, but it is unfortunate if it reflects and promotes an uncritical handling of the material.

Hidden in every method and in the philosophical outlook of the investigator are assumptions as to the nature of truth. Teachers and their students seldom face explicitly the question as to whether there are different and equally valid modes of apprehending reality. They do not often discuss the relation of such modes of apprehension to one another and their relevance to the different kinds of problems facing man. The impression that is often communicated through teaching or writing, or reports of experiments, is a positivistic one. This matter becomes especially critical as the sciences of man come to deal with the human person. As Henry A. Murray has pointed out, a split has tended to grow up between the psychological laboratory and the clinic.[7] In the lab the tendency has been toward peripheralism. The chief interest is in what is measurable. Investigations must be limited to the relatively unimportant fragments of the personality, to testing specific skills in order to get quantitative results which can be dealt with statistically. In the clinics concern is more likely to be directed to the central regions of personality, to selfhood, to man's "ambitions, frustrations, apprehensions, rages, joys, and miseries."

In other words, as Gardner Murphy has pointed out in commenting on the dominance of the experimental method within academic psychology, "the data are a function of the method used."[8] A given method is limited by its nature to a certain kind of subject matter and hence to certain kinds of conclusions with respect to that subject matter. If a method rests on an assumption implying a certain understanding of causality, the dimension of freedom and novelty may escape us, for it is but a short step from an assumption of determinism for methodological purposes to a metaphysical assertion. If a method can by nature deal only with what is common, general, abstract, it will be difficult for its user to take into account what is individual, unique, and concrete. The concreteness, the individuality, the uniqueness, of each person will escape, for example, the psychological tests which are designed to measure and compare what individuals have in common. This is the difficulty which Allport has so well stated in his contrast between the nomothetic and idiographic approaches to the study of personality.[9] It is drawn even more sharply by the existentialist critiques of rationalism in either its scientific or philosophical forms. Such views of man, taken as completely valid and encompassing interpretations, are dangerous. They fail to comprehend the limitations of their own methodology.

A further illustration of this problem is significant for the whole progress of psychology itself. In his brilliant essay on "Psychology and the Knowledge of Man," Gardner Murphy writes of the danger to the progress of psychological science of the tendency to premature integration resting on assumptions which are themselves already archaic. "What I am doubting," he writes, is "whether the thought-forms of science based on explaining the complex by reference to the supposedly simple are likely to give a sound and coherent picture of the nature of man and his place in the universe."

Just as the assumptions of the Mediterranean world are archaic, just as the assumptions of the Medieval world are archaic, so the assumptions of the seventeenth century based upon hard little particles of matter which in combining give rise to all reality, are themselves archaic. The physicalist system is archaic in biology and both the physicalist and the biological conceptions which still suffer from these assumptions, yield an archaic psychology.[10]

The difficulty arises because it is the very nature "of thought to give structure and the very nature of structured thought to reject that which does not fit in." [11] Premature integration based upon a methodology whose users are insensible to its limitations and to the nature of the assumptions which may underlie it may lead to the exclusion from consideration of much evidence which does not "fit in." The history of the sciences is full of such examples.

The point here is not to argue for a particular view of truth nor to call attention to the peculiar limitations of one or another method of investigation of psychological or social phenomena. It is to state the need for critical examination of the problem of method in relation to competence and limitation. It is to show the need for uncovering the underlying assumption about the nature of truth and reality. The issue here is related to that of the conscious or unconscious imperialism of the sciences, to the question of normative inquiry discussed earlier, and to a problem still to be discussed: namely, the matter of the relation of scientific conceptualization to the reality which it seeks to represent. Perhaps it is fair to summarize at this point by saying that wherever directly or indirectly a discipline has something to say about the nature of truth, of man's world, of man himself, that discipline touches upon issues which are of central concern to the Christian faith and to theology. Whether the contribution of a particular discipline tends to support or run counter to some theological formulation is not important. The important thing is to recognize that students and teachers alike should be aware of such issues and should attempt to meet them as competently as they are able.

Chapter V

THE CHRISTIAN TEACHER
AND THE NATURAL SCIENCES

I DO NOT KNOW HOW SATISFACTORILY MY VARIOUS ILLUSTRATIONS have communicated what I mean when I speak of the theological issues implicit in the various disciplines. This is difficult at best for those disciplines in which the subject matter comes close to the continued interests, reading, and thought of all of us. It is more difficult in those ranges of technical subject matter where few of us have any special competence, where our interest and familiarity with current discussion is even more that of laymen. Nevertheless, one of these crucial areas for both the lay and professional theologian is that of the physical and biological sciences. Here it is not so much the old issue of the relation of science and religion as it has been discussed and argued for generations, though that must not be completely neglected. Rather the issue is better represented by the comment of the historian Herbert Butterfield concerning the significance of the scientific revolution. Butterfield says that it "outshines everything since the rise of Christianity and reduces the Renaissance and the Reformation to the rank of mere episodes, mere internal displacements within the system of medieval Christendom.''[1] It is not only that science has been the chief factor in the life of modern times, but that as Whitehead has put it, more important than the new science and the new technology has been the fact that growth of science has "practically recoloured our mentality so that modes of thought which in former times were exceptional are now broadly spread throughout the educated world."[2] This transformation with all its implications for our total world view is the significant thing. It provides the context and mode of discussion for every particular issue which we may raise. Many of the latent theological issues emerge at this point quite apart from the specific problems which arise within the separate scientific disciplines.

There is no doubt that this problem appears when, on what Ernest Nagel has called ceremonial occasions, the more philosophically minded physical or biological scientist gives in to his own or someone else's desire that he deal with "ultimate questions."[3] The attempt to give an answer to the perennial "quest for a total view of the universe" is thus sometimes explicit. More often I think in the actual teaching of the sciences in liberal arts colleges it is indirect. There are off-the-cuff remarks or implicit indications of what the broader significance of the scientific enterprise and achievements are for a world view. Often, as Nagel suggests, the result is "but an echo of philosophical ideas uncritically acquired in their youth."[4] Even when there is not such a facing of the questions, there emerges out of the work of the physical and biological sciences a conception of the physical universe—a world picture which influences not only the thinking of the scientist within his particular discipline but also the thinking of all of us in other areas as well. It is of grave theological import whether the sciences can give a comprehensive view of things, becoming a sufficient substitute for metaphysics, religion, or the poet's vision. Perhaps they have only a contribution to make to our world view. This question needs to be raised by the theologian as well as the philosophers of science.[5]

The same basic question arises again in the concern the theologian has with the meaning of the scientific vision of the world. In an obvious way it is involved in the issue of the relation of scientific theory to the common experience man has of his world. Are the theoretical concepts and the objects of the sciences closer to the reality than are the ordinary everyday experiences of objects? Is the real table the one which is experienced from the perspective of the ordinary observer, or is it that which is indicated by the symbolic mathematical representations of the physicist's equations? Are these latter representations merely convenient summaries for concepts operationally defined and only valid as interpreters of reality within a particular context of investigation and discourse? What are the relations between these ways of "getting at reality"? Such questions not only are important for deciding how we are going to take the scientific world picture—whether we are going to admit other world pictures coexisting or possible of synthesis with the scientific view of the world. They are important for any other interpretation of the world (philosophical or theological) which involves cosmological speculation and metaphysical assumptions.

Equally crucial is the question of the nature and basis of reliable knowledge. This question is related to that of the nature of truth. There is of course the tendency toward imperialism, conscious or not in relation to the issue of truth, just as there is in the larger problem of world view. Many students come away from scientific studies feeling that there is but one kind of truth and one way to truth. They come to believe that this kind of truth should be sought in every area of human experience by this particular method. If such a method is inapplicable to a given area, in that area there can be no truth; there can be only opinion and subjective preference. Much the same issue is involved within the scientific disciplines themselves. As Nagel puts these questions: Is genuine knowledge absolutely certain knowledge? Is it achieved through immediate sensation, through private intellectual insight, or through some special mode of reasoning? Or is genuine knowledge within the sciences what he and Dewey would call "warranted belief"? Beneath the surface of such questions there lies the problem of the grounds for the alleged reliability of scientific knowledge. How we answer such questions carries implications for the way in which we appropriate the world picture derived from contemporary science and the way in which we relate scientific methodologies to other areas of investigation which are of such import for theology, for example, psychology, sociology, history, and so on.

Another group of problems which arises in relation to the sciences is perhaps more obviously close to the interests of religion and of the theologian. These are the problems which have to do with the relations of science to society. What conditions the rise and progress of the sciences? What are the consequences of science for the life of man apart from its practical effects for good and ill through technology? What is the meaning of the scientific enterprise—the findings of the sciences—for individual and social patterns of valuation? One might ask in a more general way whether it is possible to give a theological interpretation of the scientific enterprise as such. How is it related in its over-all historical character and its contemporary forms to the major theological problem of ultimate trust, ultimate concern, to that which sustains, nurtures, and creates human values? What light does the scientific enterprise as a whole shed upon the nature of man?

These are some of the issues arising within the sciences which have implications for the theologian or for the thinking lay Christian. Another kind of issue can be seen from within a particular scientific discipline. Here the problem is closer to those dealt with in traditional discussions of the relation of science and religion. There are dogmatists in every field of human experience and in every academic discipline. There are also those who recognize the limitations of every human perspective, who see in a conflict of interpretations both an illustration of such limitations and the possibility of a wider truth or more embracing perspective capable of reconciling the opposing views. There are those who see that there has been change and development within both theology and the sciences and that theological formulations and scientific ones as well both become dated and are culturally conditioned. There are also those among both scientists and theologians who will admit none of this. The theological issues implicit in the scientific world view or in a particular scientific discipline will be vastly different depending upon which of these attitudes we take. Personally I am convinced that Whitehead is right: "Religion will not regain its old power until it can face change in the same spirit as does science. Its principles may be eternal, but the expression of those principles requires continual development." [6]

The exponents of demythologization are right in stressing the disengagement of the religious view of life from the "adventitious notions which have crept into it by reason of the expression of its own ideas in terms of the imaginative picture of the world entertained in previous ages." [7] The sciences may help in this disengagement. They may also provide an aid thereby in promoting the communication of the fundamental experience and vision of life which religion represents. Too often our churches have been willing to interpret the meaning of religion solely in terms which are relatively incommensurable with the world of modern discourse. One must also insist, however, that ways must be found to do this without losing the essential elements in religious life and experience. From the point of view of both the Christian teacher and the student both of these aspects are of fundamental importance.

One of the obvious places within a particular discipline where there has been nearly a century of opportunity for meeting such an issue is in biology, specifically in the theory of evolution. Among Christians who recognize the need for reinterpreting religious thought in the light of empirical evidence, the challenge of the theory of evolution to traditional Christian notions of the creation of men by God, as depicted in the Genesis stories, has been accepted and has not been too difficult. Biblical studies have placed these creation stories in a new context. Changing concepts of revelation have brought an altered understanding of the role of the Bible in Christian faith. No longer is the Bible regarded primarily as a source of divinely guaranteed abstract truths about man and his world. At the same time many have recognized that myth and legend carry a kind of poetic truth which scientific abstractions cannot communicate. Others would emphasize the existential impact of the whole biblical story on those who make an effort to enter into its inner meaning.

These approaches are valuable and may help to resolve the problem of a conflict between scientific and religious interpretations of phenomena. Still more may be possible. The question would remain as to whether the Christian doctrine of creation has any relevance to the biologist's understanding of the evolution of life. Can the theologian learn anything about creation from the biologist or vice versa? Do the two modes of understanding creation meet without overlap? Do they meet and overlap to some degree without coinciding? There have been some attempts to discuss this problem, but nowhere perhaps more succinctly than in an article by the zoologist L. C. Birch, entitled "Creation and the Creator." [8] I cannot give his detailed argument here, but it may be possible to use some of the elements in his discussion to illustrate what might be involved in this and other issues involving the relationship between scientific and theological perspectives.

Birch draws attention to the difference between the views of certain theologians like Emil Brunner and those of certain Christian philosophers like Charles Hartshorne. For Brunner the Creator and his creation are distinct entities. For Hartshorne there is no such sharp distinction between the object of creation and the ever-present creativity of God. God is present in his creation as Creator, though he is not identical with his creation. If we take Brunner's view, it would follow that knowledge about the created world gained through the sciences need not inform what the Christian knows about creation through revelation. If we take Hartshorne's view, knowledge of the created world bears a direct relationship to knowledge of God's creativeness. The first view avoids a conflict between science and the Christian faith by keeping the realms of discourse separate. The second invites a conversation between the two with the possibility that both may be modified through such a conversation. In itself, of course, this difference of approach is a major issue for both the scientist who is a Christian and for the Christian theologian who is trying to relate the faith to the mind of modern man.

Birch would identify himself with the Hartshornian type of approach. He is convinced that it is undesirable to bifurcate the realm of personal experience and the re-searches of the scientist. As he puts it: "It is possible for me to say that the discovery of the processes of creation and the personal experience of redemption are mutually illuminating experiences." They are not identical, but one may shed light on the other. "The revelation of God in human experience leads to a thirst to discover the same God active in the rest of creation." [9] The question for Birch is really that which I have mentioned earlier. What is the relation of scientific conceptualization to reality it-self? Is the world a mechanism in its entirety? Can the creative process be entirely understood in mechanical terms? Are mechanical processes irrelevant to an under-standing of creation? Birch would regard the mechanistic pictures which the physicist or biologist builds as schematic representations of reality. They are models. The question is then whether you can ever get a perfect model or whether there will always be a gap between the model and the reality. To mistake the model for the reality would for

Birch be an example of Whitehead's famous fallacy of misplaced concreteness. It is the besetting sin of scientists. He would agree with scientists like Sewall Wright and Max Planck that the inner nature of reality escapes the scientific investigator. The scientist as such doesn't get beyond the model. He must recognize the limits of his experience. If he would deal with what is beyond the range of the "visible," he must be willing to venture into metaphysics. But the metaphysics he embraces cannot disregard the evidence which his scientific abstractions attempt to represent. They will tend to support or negate one or another metaphysical or metaphysically based theological interpretation of creation.

It is from such a perspective that Birch criticizes Brunner's view of creation and supports the Hartshorne—Whitehead line of thought. I shall not take the time to examine his detailed discussion. His point is clear. A study of evolutionary processes does shed light on the relationship of the Creator to creation. It even illuminates the problem of the nature of God. Theology in turn can help us to understand the way in which God is active in the creative process, for man's experience of God's redemptive activity is not utterly unlike the creative process observable in evolution. The "cross pattern" is woven into the very fabric of creation. Whatever we make of Birch's point of view or his particular arguments against Brunner or for the Hartshorne-Whitehead theory, and certainly there are other alternatives, this brief discussion will have served its purpose if it has called attention to the kind of issue over which Christian theology and a particular science may meet. Birch recognizes that the scientist as scientist need not deal with such speculative matters. He need not go beyond the model and its importance for understanding the "external aspects" of reality. As Christian, and perhaps even as man, he cannot leave his knowledge there. He wants a more complete picture of reality. But neither can he leave his scientific evidence and his scientist's picture of the world behind. He must find a synthesizing perspective which will include the scientific world view, not ignore it.

The classroom teacher in one or another of the natural sciences may well ask: "What has all this to do with what I do from day to day in class?" "Are you saying that I should introduce problems of theology or arguments for the existence of God into my class sessions?" These are legitimate questions. Let me hasten to say again what I said to the teachers of literature. The Christian teacher of the sciences ought not to "drag in" religious matters where they are irrelevant. At the same time I believe that the natural sciences taught merely as technical subject matters have no place within liberal education. The sciences themselves can be taught as liberating disciplines. They have enormous humanistic implications. These implications belong in the teaching of the sciences in our colleges. Such concerns are both legitimate and necessary in the general education in the sciences which all liberal arts students should have. They must continue to be important in the program of advanced students in the sciences if we are to become more than a nation of otherwise illiterate and irresponsible engineers and technicians. The issues I have been sketching are theological issues; they concern man and his values. They affect his interpretation of ultimate concern, his trust, his commitments. Their understanding ought to enter into the self-objectification and self-understanding of every educated man.

More than all these considerations, however, I am suggesting that the Christian teacher of the sciences, having worked through some of these issues for himself, will be teaching even his technical subject matter from a different perspective and in a different spirit. Some teachers will be more interested and better prepared than others to enter bypaths of philosophical and theological discussion, whether in or out of class, but all should be better able to communicate to students a sense of the meaning and the import of the scientific enterprise.

Chapter VI

THE CHRISTIAN TEACHER
AND METHOD

I HAVE TRIED TO SUGGEST IN THE PRECEDING DISCUSSION THAT it does make a difference whether a college or university teacher is a Christian or not. If he is a Christian, he will see and interpret his own role in a different fashion from that of even the good secular teacher. He will have a sense of *religious* vocation. He will see himself called as a Christian to lead a certain kind of life, to be a certain kind of person. He will understand his own life as a ministry—of love, forgiveness, trust, hope, light, joy, because he has come to understand and feel the significance of man's situation in terms of the self-disclosure of God in Christ. As a teacher he will feel himself called to exercise his general calling as Christian within the particular context of higher education, within the classroom as he meets students and treats his given subject matter, outside the classroom as he is a part of the college and university community. As a Christian teacher he will, I think, as I have tried to indicate, handle his own discipline somewhat differently than if he has made no Christian commitment. There will be a self-consciousness about issues which are important both within his particular discipline itself and for his students' movement toward maturity. He will be interested in certain kinds of relevance which even the best secular teacher might well ignore or be unconcerned about. He will be concerned to "play fair" with religion within his own discipline, to make clear to the student the significant part that religion has played and does play in the life of men individually and culturally. He will want the student to be able to recognize the deeper theological issues which are at stake within every academic discipline. He will be concerned to help his students see that a religious interpretation of human existence, indeed a Christian one, is both a possible one and an intellectually respectable one. He will not regard himself as a propagandist for the Christian faith or for a particular formulation of it, nor will he violate his responsibilities as a scholar or the integrity of his students. Perhaps in relation to the content of what he teaches he can do no more.

With respect to methods of teaching and of relating to students, new considerations enter in. My own conviction is that a Christian teacher who thinks the matter through will be seriously concerned with the problem of educational method. He will, of course, want to be the most effective teacher he can be, and this would be ground enough for a concern with method. But he will also be aware that much more is communicated through one's method of teaching than the particular subject matter with which he deals. This "more" will be a matter for serious attention. The teacher-student relationship is one kind of interpersonal relationship. Like all other interpersonal relationships it is heavily weighted with possibilities for good or ill for its participants. The realm of the interpersonal is perhaps the most crucial of the areas of experience through which each one of us forms his own view of himself and his world. It is the area in which the basic feeling for life and the direction of self-realization is shaped. Here if anywhere in the teaching profession there is the opportunity for the teacher to realize his sense of vocation as a ministry, a ministry of love, forgiveness, trust, hope, light, and joy. Here is the opportunity, within the limitations of a teacher-student relationship, to provide conditions conducive to personal growth. Here in a context of freedom, judgment, and love some contribution can be made toward giving each individual the kinds of experiences which may become a personal resource for understanding his own life and the human situation generally in Christian terms. I should first like to address the Christian teacher's concern with educational method from the point of view of effective teaching itself, recognizing that even here there are theological presuppositions and implications involved in the questions of how persons learn and what the most effective methods of teaching are. I should then like to consider the "more" which is involved in the teaching process, a "more" which, since it concerns the shaping and forming of personal life, will be a deep concern to the Christian teacher.

Probably there are few teachers in our colleges and universities who have given very much thought to teaching method. There is a kind of disparagement of concern with method which has grown out of a reaction against the over-emphasis on technique at the expense of subject matter in some of our teachers' colleges and schools of education. There is too I think, some defensiveness involved in the response that college teachers give to those who would bring the problem of method to the fore. Most of us are willing to engage in discussions of goals and aims of education, of revising curricula, and the like, but we do not care to subject our teaching methods to careful scrutiny. Yet as Sidney Hook has pointed out, all plans for educational reform depend on the teacher for their proper realization.[1] It may be that notwithstanding changes in curricula or reformulation of educational aims we produce men no more competent or responsible than did our predecessors fifty or a hundred years ago. Our students in some disciplines may have more technical proficiency, but are they more responsible human beings? I am inclined to think that many of our graduates might agree with the comment Dexter Keezer made when he went to Reed College as president.[2] Though Keezer thought that the teaching at Reed was extraordinarily good in its line, he was equally struck by the fact that there had been little change of any kind in teaching methods since his own college days, in spite of enormous potentialities for such improvement. He pointed out that he found that college teachers were relatively uninterested in how to teach because they thought that subject matter was so much more important than the methods they used. Many of us who are familiar with the educational scene might also agree with Hook's statement that the most satisfactory teaching in American education is done at the elementary level and the least satisfactory at the highest level. Hook writes: "Practices are countenanced in colleges which would not be suffered for one moment in any good elementary or secondary high school."[3] Confirmation of our own failure comes to us when we reflect that so often what seems to be learned bears little relation to what we thought we taught.

There is real reason then to be concerned with what our

way of teaching contributes to the learning of the student. If we would maximize learning and make that learning significant, such understanding becomes critical. Beyond the facilitation of the learning of a particular subject matter some of us may conclude as did Henry Seidel Canby: "What I tried to teach was never so important as how I taught it." [4] Or with Gordon Allport we may say that "what is taught turns out in the long run to be less important than the manner of teaching." [5] What Allport means and what so often escapes many of us is the fact that controlling attitudes, formative impressions, fundamental purposes, and the direction or thrust of one's life as a whole may be a most important part of what is appropriated out of the particular mode of teaching as well as out of the subject matter.

What all teachers need and what Christian teachers must have in relation to the question of method is a self-consciousness about the issue, a willingness to examine one's own teaching methods, and a lack of defensiveness about the problem of method in general. Dogmatism is out of the question here. Those "experts" are probably wrong who would claim that there is one or another teaching method which is superior to every other. Those are equally wrong who assume that the old methods—lecture, or tutorial, or classroom recitation—need no critical examination or improvement. Certainly a man must adopt the teaching methods which he can use best; he must use the methods which are best for his subject matter; he must evaluate method in relation to the kind of student he teaches. To make the best choice under given circumstances demands not only self-examination but also a study of the relation of particular methods to particular educational goals, to specific subject matter, and to types of students. It demands a willingness to experiment and observe the results. It demands an awareness of the newer methods of teaching and variations on the older methods. It demands acquaintance with the studies of the effectiveness of various teaching methods.

One of the most refreshing things a teacher can do is to read some of the more thoughtful discussions of teaching such as Gilbert Highet's *The Art of Teaching* or Houston Peterson's *Great Teachers*. If he can consider his own work critically in the light of such reading, he will have made a great step forward. He can do more than this. Together with like-minded individuals in his own faculty he can discuss and experiment with teaching method. They can familiarize themselves with some of the experiments in teaching which have already been made. These experiments not only may be directly helpful, but they may provoke a willingness to experiment and stimulate an awareness of issues which might otherwise go unnoticed. I should like to call attention to several such studies of the teaching process.

The reports of Nathaniel Cantor's experiments with teaching method are most easily accessible in his two books *The Dynamics of Learning* and *The Teaching-Learning Process*. Both of these books start from the premise that the student must do his own learning. Crucial to learning is the student's attitude toward the various factors of the learning process: toward himself, the teacher, his fellow students, the subject matter, the classroom atmosphere. Personal factors are seen to be a the core of the teaching-learning process. The basic problem according to Cantor is to devise situations which will evoke student interest, participation, and self-responsibility. It is the problem not so much of what is taught as of how the student is to learn. What is of greatest importance is the student's perception of himself and his situation, not the objective situation or the objective knowledge which is to be communicated. Cantor's point of view is sustained by the kind of phenomenological psychology represented by Snygg's and Combs's *Individual Behavior*, by the work of men like Carl Rogers. Something akin to it is implicit in the remark of Whitehead that the attempt to treat the mind as a passive receiver or an instrument to be sharpened is "one of the most fatal, erroneous, and dangerous conceptions ever introduced into the theory of education." [6]

Because of his recognition of the importance of the student's perception of self and situation in the learning process, Cantor is deeply concerned with taking these factors into account in the actual teaching process. An example is his analysis of the significance of classroom atmosphere. Cantor has found in experimenting through his own teaching that the learner learns better and learns what is of importance to him if he does not feel defensive, if he is not threatened. He learns best when he is free to "face his uncertainties, limitations, and inadequacies." [7] Learning can be increased therefore by creating an atmosphere of acceptance in which the individual can accept himself as well as others and the teacher. Cantor tries to develop the feeling tone which will encourage students to "question, challenge, and contribute to one another's and the teacher's growth." [8]

Much more is involved of course than this, but the function of the teacher is to create the most favorable conditions for learning, recognizing that this means taking account of the student's perception of himself and his situation. The student learns best when he is free from the fear of authority, from lowered self-esteem, from a feeling of insignificance. He is then released to express himself, his differences, his disagreement. As Harry Stack Sullivan has clearly shown, persons through what he calls "selective inattention" [9] become closed to experience which could otherwise be a valued learning experience. They have eyes to see, but they see not, and ears to hear, but they hear not. Such selective inattention is the result of disrupting anxiety. In relation to the problem of education Sullivan has made the wise remark: The worst method of educating children is to create anxiety in them; the second worst method is not to generate *any* anxiety in them.

Perhaps my own experience in college teaching may shed some light on this problem. Some years prior to reading Cantor's study of the teaching process, I stumbled upon an approach which is not unlike his. I was concerned with helping students become more highly motivated in their learning and with discovering ways of developing critical skills and attitudes which would be carried beyond the classroom and the time of formal education. I had been impressed with what had been done in adult education with the Great Books program. My idea was to devise a course in which controversial issues could be studied, but studied in such a fashion that large responsibility could be thrown upon the students themselves. The course which finally emerged centered around topics central to anyone's philosophy of life: the meaning of education, the aims and goals of the economic and political orders, a philosophy of marriage and the family, the place of creativeness in the life of man whether through hobbies, or art, music, and literature, the meaning of religion. Each student was required to construct in outline form a systematic presentation of his views on each of these topics. Taken as a whole his papers represented his "philosophy of life" at that time.

The class sessions were given over to discussion of the most provocative essays and books I could find, representing contrasting points of view on each of the topics. No lectures were given. Everyone was allowed to express his own viewpoint, to challenge or question those of other class members. At the beginning of the term I found it necessary to start the discussion and from time to time to keep it moving without too much wandering away from the central concern, but little by little the students came to sense the spirit of the enterprise, to take more and more responsibility for both the direction and the success of the venture, until finally I became less and less the initiator and director of the process and more of a fellow participant in a continuing dialectic.

It is difficult to communicate the difference in the spirit of this kind of class or the progressive movement in self-expression and self-exploration. From a period of initial hesitancy and some anxiety the class moved toward an alert and yet relaxed dialogue of mind and feeling. What could be objectively measured was the great increase in a sense of responsibility for one's own learning, the moving beyond the assigned responsibilities in reading and writing, the genuine enthusiasm for wrestling with the intellectual issues, carried on well beyond the class hour, and the changed attitude toward themselves and other participants. In reflecting on the experience one of the students put into words a sentiment which found agreement among the other class members: "For the first time I felt that I was treated as a mature person."

Teachers may not take over Cantor's approach to teaching as a whole, but they can surely learn a great deal from it. They may be led to re-examine their own teaching in relation to the anxiety it creates, to the self-perception and situational perception of the students, to the residual learning that is left after facts and theories which make up the immediate and detailed learning have been forgotten. They may be ready to look at their own teaching in light of the thesis that it is the student who learns, that quality and degree of participation govern in large part what is learned. The same emphasis on participation as a mode of learning is made by those who are using a case method approach to teaching. Teaching by the case method is of course not possible in all of the disciplines, but it has been widely used and it may be possible to devise new uses in dealing with materials which as first do not seem to lend themselves to such treatment. The method has been fruitfully used in medicine, law, social service, ethics, and business administration.

One of the most interesting accounts of this approach to learning is to be found in a book edited by K. R. Andrews entitled *The Case Method of Teaching Human Relations and Administration*.[10] This book recounts the experience of the faculty at the Harvard Graduate School of Business Administration. Mastery of facts or of cut and dried solutions to a number of typical problems, whether such information is communicated through lectures or reading, was felt to be an inadequate training for the modern business leader. What was needed was the preparation of students for independent thinking and responsible action where there is no "right" answer, no easily applicable principle which can be learned and readily applied. A case, as these men use the term, "is a record of a business issue which *actually* has been faced by business executives, together with surrounding facts, opinions, and prejudices upon which executive decisions have to depend." [11] Such a case is presented for analysis, open discussion, and final decision as to what type of action should be taken. The aim of this method of teaching is to develop the student's ability "to act in a mature fashion under conditions of responsibility"; the temptation is for the teacher to tell what he knows, to point out what he believes to be the right answer in terms of thought and action. Such a procedure would be unlikely to improve the student's own insight or make him better able to meet novel situations under conditions of responsibility. Properly used, these teachers believe, the case system "initiates students into ways of independent thought and responsible judgment."

It faces them with situations which are not hypothetical but real. It places them in the active role, open to criticism from all sides. It puts the burden of understanding and judgment upon them. It provides them with the occasion to deal constructively with their contemporaries and their elders. And, at least in the area of business, it gives them the stimulating opportunity to make contributions to learning.[12]

The point here again is that the student must do his own learning. The teacher's task is to provide the conditions under which he can do his own learning. "We cannot effectively use the insight and knowledge of others; it must be our own knowledge and insight that we use." [13]

Not only is the content differently organized in this use of the case method, but the role of teacher and student is altered from that of traditional modes of teaching. Students accustomed to other ways of teaching may first react by wanting facts and ideas handed to them. They want the answers. When they find that the answers are not given, they pass through a period of confusion and of feeling help-less. Later they come to accept the need for co-opera-tive working on problems easily and without fear. Finally they come to recognize that the instructors do not always know the "best answers," and even when they do the stu-dent can still hold his own views. As Dean Donham has written: "The essential fact which makes the case system ... an educational method of the greatest power is that it arouses the interest of the student by making him an active rather than a passive participant." [14]

I have experimented from time to time with adaptations of the case method of teaching and am willing to give testi-mony in support of Dean Donham's contention. One such venture centered in a course in ethical theory. In place of a straightforward analysis and presentation of various ethi-cal theories, I attempted to combine such a procedure with case analysis. Plays, novels, and various real life situations were read, representing cases full of unresolved ethical issues. The class was then faced with the problem of analy-sis and interpretation. How would a Spinoza or a Dewey interpret this situation? What elements would go into the making of an ethical decision in this case from the point of view of a Schweitzer or a Macmurray. Finally after clari-fying the ethical issues from one or another point of view, each student was asked to present his own solution to the dilemma together with an analysis of the underlying pre-suppositions on the basis of which he seemed to be coming to a decision. The liveliness of the discussion, the relatively greater success in mastering the skills of ethical analysis, the retention and the capacity to understand the implications of classical ethical theory, as well as the amount of self-understanding which emerged from this kind of teaching have been hard to match in my experience.

Another series of studies directly related to the problem of the connection between participation and learning have been made at the University of Chicago. In one of these studies there has been a direct investigation of the conditions of learning in a classroom situation. Most of us have wondered at one time or another what was going on in the students' minds as we lectured or carried on a discussion. By an ingenious method Professor B. S. Bloom and his associates have been able to present a fairly clear picture of what it is students think about under these conditions.[15] He has been able to measure the degree of covert and overt participation and the relevance of such participation to achievement in learning. Bloom found, for example, not only that students may participate either overtly or covertly but that a student's achievement is highly correlated to participation of both kinds. Most student thinking can be traced to stimuli in the classroom environment. It is particularly stimulated by the verbal activity of the teacher and the other students, but some of it is irrelevant to the subject under discussion. Bloom's results show clearly that the nature of the method used for instruction determines the *kind* of thinking done. He found that more than one third of student thinking going on during a lecture is directly related to following the lecturer. In discussion sections only one fifth of the student thinking was bent on following the course of the discussion. More than 60 per cent of the thinking in lecture sessions was directly related to the subject at hand, 55 per cent in the discussion sections. His conclusion is that there is less irrelevent thinking in relation to the lecture method. The great difference, however, was that thinking in lecture sessions was more passive while in the discussion sessions it was much more active and problem solving. A good deal of thinking under both types of instruction was irrelevant to the subject at hand. Much of it was concerned with the student himself and other persons. Bloom recognizes the need for centering instruction in the student, for taking account of his anxieties and difficulties, and for providing a supportive classroom environment. Where one is interested in promoting the kind of learning in which active problem solving is essential, one type of method will be best. Where the teacher simply wants the assimilation of facts, another type will be best.

This conclusion is supported in a further investigation of the discussion method of teaching and learning carried on by some of the same researchers at the University of Chicago.[16] The investigation was of a preliminary kind. It was directed toward determining the extent to which a discussion method was capable of bringing about the achievement of the college's educational aims. In its stated educational aims the college held that

knowledge worth the name must be more than a memory of facts and of favored interpretations of facts. It involves an understanding of the ways in which facts are acquired and the processes of reasoning by which they have been interpreted. All real knowledge includes a grasp of reasons.[17]

The group of investigators then proceeded to study what actually went on in different kinds of class discussions in order to see what particular ways of handling discussion were most fruitful in helping the student to achieve such educational aims. The key to learning of this kind was held to be the degree to which the student himself organizes what he learns as against learning material that is pre-organized. "Organize" here means relating to what has previously been known by the individual or the formation of it into a new relational pattern. In a carefully devised scheme for analyzing a large number of actual class discussions, certain patterns of student behavior, of teacher attitude, and method of handling discussion came to be distinguished. Arranged on a continuum these elements provide a means for evaluating the degree to which the particular educational aims of this particular college will be met. The points on the continuum can be summarized as follows:[18]

1. The student listens to the instructor expound a point.
2. The student asks questions in order to clarify in his own mind what the instructor has said.
3. The student challenges the instructor's statements.
4. The student propounds his own solution to a problem and has it approved or corrected by the instructor; if corrected, he listens to the instructor's reasons for modifying or rejecting.
5. The student propounds his own solution to a problem and is led by the instructor to elaborate and to defend it against attack, to relate it to other ideas, to modify it, if necessary, in the light of the attacks, and so on.
6. The student participates in a group effort in which number 5 is done by other students as well as by himself.

From the perspective of those who hold the aims of this college a set of procedures will probably be "better" as it calls forth in the student an increasingly larger amount of the kind of behavior represented in the continuum as one moves downward.

The point of the investigators is not simply that different methods of instruction and of handling discussion will differ in their success for achieving particular educational goals, but that teachers with insight into their own behavior and understanding of the elements important for such success can modify their behavior, their attitudes, and actually improve their teaching effectiveness markedly. While I believe any college teacher will find this study of *Teaching by Discussion* profitable reading on its own account, my real reason for describing the report is to call attention to the importance and the possibility of looking at particular methods critically in relation to specific educational aims. This is an area in college teaching in which much needs to be done. The individual teacher does not have to wait for some group of educational "experts" to make a study; he can begin with his own teaching.

Chapter VII

THE DEEPER IMPLICATIONS
OF METHOD

I HAVE BEEN TALKING ABOUT THE CHRISTIAN TEACHER'S CON-cern with educational method. I have said he takes his teaching with pre-eminent seriousness. He wants to be the best teacher he can. His sense of responsibility is not simply derived from his interest in students or in education or in a discipline but is grounded in his own relation to God. His concern with the intellectual, the academic in the narrow sense, with minds and subject matter, is rooted in his own sense of religious vocation. Yet at the same time he knows that man is not mind alone and that mastery of a particular subject matter is not all there is to education. There is a deeper learning which goes on concurrently with the mastery of a discipline, a learning which in many respects is beyond the intent and control of the teacher. In all that I have said and in all that I will say about teaching and learning, this deeper teaching and deeper learning have been in my mind. Perhaps the clearest way to state what I mean is to point to what I call the dimensional character of the teaching-learning process.

The phenomenon of learning ranges from the simple to the complex. On one level there is the learning of skills and information. On another level there is the acquisition of attitudes and values. On still another level there is the fundamental transformation of personal orientation. Some learning seems to focus predominantly in one or another of these dimensions. It is clear, however, that they are often and perhaps always interrelated so that even the learning of a new skill or a new bit of information or a new idea affects attitudes and to some degree personal orientation.

I first became fully aware of the significance of these distinctions in my own teaching. I began to notice a radical difference in effect between two kinds of courses I was teaching. I came to see that one type of course brought a great deal of personal involvement, that it sometimes brought about a radical kind of change or reorientation in some students. The other kind of course, as I began to analyze it, seemed to be focused chiefly on the communication of information and ideas. The first type of course put issues before students in such a way that they had to take a stand. They had to make decisions. The second type of course required only that the student absorb the information and give evidence that he had understood the ideas which had been communicated. The difference was not simply one between activity and passivity on the student's part. To be sure, the student could more easily be passive in the "information type" course, but he could be active too. He could busy himself with the study of other people's ideas, with the assimilation of facts, with the comparison of various perspectives and viewpoints. I came to think of the chief difference between the two ways of teaching as a difference between an existential and a nonexistential approach. An existential approach involves the student—makes him take a stand, forces him to decision. He must stake himself. A non-existential approach allows him to remain aloof, to memorize and repeat, to master other men's opinions, to criticize and compare, but always objectively—without becoming involved as a total person. It became clear to me that not all subject matters lend themselves equally well to an existential approach, and yet where they do, a deeper and more lasting kind of education seems to take place.

As a layman in the natural sciences I have wondered a good deal whether what I have called the existential approach was adaptable in the teaching of physics or chemistry or biology at least at the elementary levels. Certainly the natural scientist engaged in research must be involved, must make decisions, must interpret evidence which may point in a number of directions. But even laboratory science at the elementary levels if it is to be more than repeating experiments "by the handbook" and making the answers come out the way they are supposed to come out can escape the educational travesty of simply learning someone else's opinions. The vivid account recorded by Shaler of his initial study under Louis Agassiz stands in my mind as an example of existential teaching in the sciences, which, if it is not to be directly imitated, certainly points toward some of the goals of what I have called deeper teaching.

Shaler was assigned a small pine table with a rusty tin pan upon it in Agassiz's primitive laboratory and museum. He tells his story as follows:

When I sat me down before my tin pan, Agassiz brought me a small fish, placing it before me with the rather stern requirement that I should study it, but should on no account talk to any one concerning it, nor read anything relating to fishes until I had his permission to so do. To my inquiry, "What shall I do?" he said in effect, "Find out what you can without damaging the specimen; when I think that you have done the work I will question you." In the course of an hour I thought I had compassed the fish; it was rather an unsavory object, giving forth the stench of old alcohol, then loathsome to me, though in time I came to like it. Many of the scales were loosened so that they fell off. It appeared to me to be a case of a summary report, which I was anxious to make and get on to the next stage of the business. But Agassiz, though always within call, concerned himself no further with me that day, nor the next, nor for a week. At first, this neglect was distressing; but I saw that it was a game, for he was, as I discerned rather than saw, covertly watching me. So I set my wits to work upon the thing, and in the course of a hundred hours or so thought I had done much—a hundred times as much as seemed possible at the start. I got interested in finding out how the scales went in series, their shape, the form and placement of the teeth, etc. Finally, I felt full of the subject and probably expressed it in my bearing; as for words about it then, there were none from my master except his cheery "Good morning." At length on the seventh day, came the question "Well?" and my disgorge of learning to him as he sat on the edge of my table puffing his cigar. At the end of the hour's telling, he swung off and away, saying, "That is not right." Here I began to think that after all perhaps the rules for scanning Latin verse were not the worst infliction in the world. Moreover, it was clear that he was playing a game with me to find if I were capable of doing hard, continuous work without the support of a teacher, and this stimulated me to labor. I went at the task anew, discarded my first notes, and in another week of ten hours a day labor I had results which astonished myself and satisfied him.[1]

Shaler goes on with his story of his education under Louis Agassiz, revealing through his own words how much more great teaching does than create competent technicians or knowledge of the facts and theories of a given discipline.

The point of my remarks on the dimensional character of the teaching-learning process can be simply summarized: the methods used in teaching have important effects beyond facilitating the communication of a particular subject matter. They affect the formation of attitudes in the student; they do more—they play an important part in determining the kind of person the student is to become. This aspect of the problem of method will therefore be of grave concern to the Christian teacher.

We do not know very much about these "by-products" of the teaching process, though it is evident from the recollections and reports of those who have studied under some of the great teachers that they are of enormous importance. The influence of the great teacher is felt far beyond the range of his competence in communicating his particular subject matter. Lives are changed in and through teaching and teachers. This we know. Just how, under what circumstances, and in what ways is not precisely understood. Allowing for a considerable range of possible interpretation, some guesses may be undertaken.

What, for example, is the effect of authoritarian teaching on the individual student and indirectly on the culture and social order through the influence of these students? The answer is not clear since individuals will be affected differently by such teaching, depending upon their own personality structures and the other forces impinging upon them. Some may resist or rebel. In others authoritarian teaching may produce conformity, thwart the development of independence of spirit and judgment. We know that the kind of personal being formed through authoritarian situations whether of family, in education, or in some other context does tend to reproduce itself. The authoritarian man may be subservient to all authority, or he may reproduce in his relations to others the dominance-submission pattern on those below him in the order of prestige, power, and status. Neither form of the "authoritarian man," the submissive or the dominating individual, represents the Christian image of man. If we would have our educational process help produce men and women who are centers of freedom and love, who can enter into relationships with others freely and in mutual respect, neither an authoritarian family pattern nor an authoritarian method of teaching is the way to bring it about.

Everything that we do in relation to the student—our way of stating issues, our method of correcting him, our willingness or unwillingness to take seriously what he sees, feels, or thinks—helps to shape the picture which he has of himself. What we allow to go on in the classroom or the seminar does the same. And the image which the student has of himself not only affects his capacity to learn a particular subject matter, but it influences, often to a considerable degree, the kind of person he becomes. We have heard again and again that man is a social being. In this instance the meaning is that we interpret ourselves in the light of what we believe others to think and feel about us. The student who is the butt of sarcasm or irony or humiliation, the student who is made the object of ridicule by teacher or fellows, may be strong enough in himself or through other supporting influences to maintain a self-idea which is healthful and releasing. He may on the other hand be bludgeoned into withdrawal; he may come to feel so worthless that his potentialities may be sharply reduced; he may become twisted and warped in ways which affect his relationships to all others and his total orientation to life in an unwholesome and negative way.

There are other by-products of various methods of teaching. Madeleine P. Grant tells of one of her students in biology who had done some original work on the process of bone formation in the chick embryo. She was scheduled to exhibit her study before a meeting of the Anatomists' Association. The teacher could recall the student's intellectual excitement over her project, but what the student remembered out of the experience was her own struggle with self-discipline. Some time afterward she commented that what she valued most in college was having had to finish this study. It was this aspect of her work which she recalled most vividly. Another student, some years later when she had become a successful physician, looked back on her comparative anatomy course. What stood out in her mind was what the teacher had said about her attitude toward her own abilities.[2] Student comments years after their learning experience are difficult to assess, yet each of us knows from his own experience that one or another teacher has contributed far more to his life and to the development of values and character than the content of the particular discipline which has been under study.

The teacher himself is one of these imponderables. Method is not mere technique. It is the whole process of communication with its overtones and its undertones. The teacher's enthusiasm for his subject, his openness to or his rejection of the views and opinions of others, his serious concern with scholarship, his willingness to revise his own judgments and to make connections between his subject matter and the wider ranges of other areas of learning and life, are some of the factors which affect the communication which is the teaching-learning process.

We know that each stage of development in the life span of an individual from early years to old age has its characteristic problems and crisis situations. Some of these are brought about largely by cultural demands, others by biological changes in the organism. The way in which the individual meets the particular issues of life in any one period of his development not only facilitates or thwarts his development in succeeding stages; it has repercussions throughout all the areas of his life. One of the chief problems of adolescence centers around the development of a sense of identity. The college student is working through the resolution of this crucial developmental task. He is trying to come to terms with himself. He is trying to bring together his own view of himself and the impression he thinks others have of him. He is trying to synthesize his own hopes and expectations with the hopes and expectations others have for him. Much of what the teacher is and does in relation to the student affects the student's achievement of this sense of identity. In dealing with the specific materials of a course, in entering into personal relations with the teacher and his fellow students, a student is moving toward a basic resolution of his probelm. Earlier adolescence tends to get its sense of identity through particular individuals. The boy or girl identifies with a particular "hero." Sometimes even a college student may make this kind of identification with a teacher. "This is the kind of man or woman I want to be." Or negatively, "This is the kind of man or woman I do not want to be." More typically, however, the late adolescent, though very much influenced by particular adults, is relatively critical and sophisticated about his identifications. He is more likely to make a conscious and unconscious selection of characteristics which in their own emerging pattern help to solidify his sense of role or to integrate the various roles which he presently sees or envisages himself as playing. Such a movement toward a sense of personal identity more often than not is a movement which sets the direction for the future. It charts the path and gives the guiding image for a good part of the later life of the individual.

Teachers cannot avoid playing a role in relation to this developing sense of self-identity. They should be aware of this role even though they can neither predict nor control it. The role is part of what has been called the "terrible responsibility of the teacher." Even though it is played in relation to the sphere of freedom of the student, a sensitive teacher can cultivate an awareness of the quality of his own contribution to this process. He may be able to exert some constructive influence or to eliminate or ameliorate some of the dangerous and disintegrating elements in the process.

If it is important to call attention to the part that teachers play as individuals in the shaping of the lives and attitudes of students, it is equally important to point to other factors in the teaching-learning situation which have a similar impact. Particularly significant in certain teaching-learning contexts are the roles played by the other students. Both subject matter learning and the other kinds of learning which inevitably accompany it are affected by the kind and quality of the interaction within the class. A sense of self-identity may sometimes be shaped quite as much by the reciprocal relations of one class member to the others as it is by his relations to the teacher. Whether the group is open, democratic, co-operative, or split by conflict, competition, patterns of dominance and submission, will help to determine how any individual participant comes to think of himself and evaluate himself. Does he come to see himself as a creative, responsible member of an inquiring group, independent in some ways and interdependent in others? Or does he come to see himself as a passive and dependent or aggressive and competitive partisan either of his own interests or of some party within or outside the classroom? What I have spoken of broadly as the teacher's method has something to do with the answers to such questions. The texture of human relationships within the learning situation, the over-all atmosphere, though they are almost intangible and very difficult to assess with precision, are yet pervasive, influential, sometimes even decisive in the making of a student's mind or person.

On crossing the campus one time, I overheard one freshman saying to another as they came out of class together: "The more I learn here, the more I want to learn everything there is to know around this university." This comment came only three weeks after the beginning of term. What had to happen in a class to stir up such excitement and eagerness to learn in a new student? What kind of atmosphere for teaching and learning would have to be maintained to keep such enthusiasm alive? How would one keep alive this student's picture of himself as a learner for whom there need be no stopping point, no boundaries to the life of a scholar?

This sketch of the importance of method for the Christian teacher would not be complete without some recognition of the limitations of the situation in which many teachers carry on their work. Some teachers are faced by classes of huge size. Others are under pressure to cover a predetermined body of material within a specified time in order to fulfill requirements for specialized vocational or professional programs. The absence of genuinely selective admissions policies in an institution brings into some classes many students who are so ill-prepared, or unmotivated, or intellectually incompetent, as to be unable to carry on a college level program of study. There are in addition the pressures of extra-curricular activities, many of which have genuine educational value, felt by almost all our students. These compete for the students' time and attention. Such factors need to be taken into account, but they do not, it seems to me, undercut the validity of what I have been saying about method. Some of these basic principles apply to large classes as well as to small, and in many cases it will be both desirable and possible to section large courses into smaller groups for at least part of the time. Even with large courses it is possible to be concerned with the atmosphere which is being created, with the context in which learning is going on. A teacher can present material in ways which challenge a student to do his own thinking, to take a stand. Whether we are teaching a dozen students or two hundred, we can consider how our way of stating issues, our attitude toward the subject matter, our openness or rejection of the views of others, may affect the attitudes of students both toward learning and toward themselves. Whether or not we make an effort to make connections between our studies and wider ranges of learning and other areas of life does not depend finally on the kind of limitations which have been cited.

It is true, of course, that some circumstances may make it impossible to have much personal give and take with many students as individuals. It may still, however, be possible to make the whole approach more person centered than it might otherwise be. Even though he cannot take into account the peculiar situation of individual students, a teacher can still keep before his eyes, as he teaches the qualities, interests, and problems of various kinds of students. Nor is the possibility of experimenting with method utterly destroyed by some of these limiting factors. The use of case materials or the development of various kinds of small groups within the framework of a large course, for example, may still be tried. Experiments with self-organizing, independent, student-led groups may prove exceptionally productive. One student tells of his experience in a large course in criminology which was broken up into many working committees of two and three students each. "This course produced the most personal involvement and the most self-initiated learning of all my courses at the university," he writes. Teachers faced by factors which seriously limit their control of the teaching-learning situation may well find their ingenuity put to the test and great demands made upon their creativity. It is doubtless the part of wisdom to face realistically such limitations but at the same time not to give the situation up as hopeless. Nevertheless, the difficulties put in the way of really effective teaching at some institutions may be so great that the genuinely committed teacher, Christian or non-Christian, may be bound to protest such threats to the goals which he believes higher education is meant to serve. Such teachers may continue to work within the given framework, but they may be justifiably moved to band together with like-minded colleagues to better the situation both for their own sakes and for the students whom they serve.

Chapter VIII

UNDERSTANDING THE STUDENTS

NEXT TO HIS INTEREST IN AND HIS COMPETENT GRASP OF HIS
subject matter the most important factor in the work of
the Christian teacher is an interest in and an understanding
of the students with whom he works. Understanding the
student is closely related to the problem of method, since an
effective application of any method of teaching depends on
knowing the student and knowing how he learns. It not only
is one of the keys to good teaching, but it is also the key
to communicating the Christian faith in action. Teaching is
communication. Sometimes it is direct communication;
sometimes the communication is indirect. In both cases the
success of the communication depends in part on understanding the individual or the group to whom you are trying to communicate. Some teachers seem to have a natural
understanding of students. They remember enough of how
the world seemed to them as adolescents to be able to project themselves imaginatively into the world of their students. Others have enough sensitivity and openness to grasp
what is going on in the students to whom their teaching
must be relevant if anything is to be learned. Many of the

rest of us are aware of a kind of abyss between ourselves and our students fostered by a difference of age, interest, and common experience. All of us can make our teaching more effective as we become aware of the motivations, interests, resources, and problems of our students.

There are two levels of understanding the student. One must understand the student "in general," and one must understand the individual student. The first kind of understanding will increase one's capacity to understand the individual. Understanding individual students will give insight into the student "in general." It is quite obvious, of course, that there is no student "in general." There is nothing which can accurately be called the student mind. There are, however, certain basic problems and characteristic patterns of experience shared by most American college students. There are types of students. The longer we teach, the more easily we recognize these and learn how to deal with them. Yet no student fully fits a type or shares completely the characteristic pattern of experience. We have to be aware of uniqueness even in working with groups of students. At the same time it is worth while making a deliberate attempt to be sensitive to the distinctive characteristics, problems, experience, and interests which students share. We need to know what I call the "existence situation" out of which and in which the student learns whatever he does learn.

We need, for example, to be aware of the sociocultural factors which shape the life and attitudes of our students, for intellectual capacity is hardly the only factor which conditions the academic success of our students.[1] In the past most of our students have come from upper or lower middle class backgrounds. Many of our colleges are operated on the assumptions that their students will have "middle class values, habits, and vocational experiences." It seems now that a drastic shift is going on in the composition of student populations. A larger and larger proportion of students are coming from working-class homes. These home backgrounds give the students "different expectations in life, different values, different manners and mores." These facts are not irrelevant to effective teaching, since they affect not only student motivation and goals but the kind of problem the student faces in his learning and in his total adjustment to the college situation. They affect the image which he has of himself. Various typologies might be designed to distinguish the students in terms of their sociocultural background. One such classification speaks of the "high status statics," the "climbers," and the "strainers." The high status statics are good risks; these are students of upper or upper middle socioeconomic classes; they have the typical educational attitudes of their social group. The climbers come from the lower middle or working-class youth; they have a real ambition to get ahead in life. They have friends among students of higher social status; they pick up their attitudes toward education. With good minds and strong personalities they can exert the self-control and do the hard work necessary for success. Yet even for the climber there are situations in which he may be ruined. He needs a situation in which he can develop socially, where social lines are not too exclusive or drawn too tightly. His efforts and his virtues need to be rewarded and encouraged. The strainer, on the other hand, may be a poor risk in any situation. Coming from the lower middle or working class, he has mixed goals. His personality is vacillating. He wants to make good, but he is "not sure yet what this means." He makes friends with students of higher social backgrounds, but he is not sure that he wants their way of life. Such students have need for educational guidance and understanding beyond that needed for the other two types. For each of these types learning comes to focus in a different context. The teacher may be much more effective if he is aware of the background factors which condition the learning of his students and if he takes into account the subtle influence of his own class backgrounds and attitudes.

There are common experiences and common problems which transcend the differentia of sociocultural backgrounds, though these too may be shaped by such factors. By virtue of their common biological development and the common social demands laid upon them in our culture, college students share characteristic developmental tasks. A developmental task has been defined as a "task which arises at or about a certain period in the life of the individual, successful achievement of which leads to his happiness and to success with later tasks, while failure leads to unhappiness in the individual, disapproval by the society, and difficulty with later tasks." [2] College teaching takes place in relation to individuals who are facing the common developmental tasks of late adolescence, who are carrying with them the success or failure in their earlier developmental tasks, and who are oriented toward the developmental tasks of early adulthood. "If the task is not achieved at the proper time it will not be achieved well, and failure in this task will cause partial or complete failure in the achievement of other tasks yet to come." [3] When we try to teach a subject to students, we are not dealing just with their intellects. Intellectual behavior and learning are an aspect of the life of the whole person, shaped, conditioned, catalyzed, or frustrated by what is happening in the life of the whole person. The success, the failures, the anxieties, the stress, in these other areas of life are, as we know full well in the case of the failing student, of immense importance in the learning of all students. This notion of developmental task is one of the ways in which we can get at an understanding of the world of our students. Any one of us who is close to adolescent life knows in his own way elements of the students' life which reflect their wrestling with these tasks. We know the power of group approval in the lives of our students, the struggle of the individual with the question "Am I normal?" the difficulties that many students have with their parents and that their parents have with them. We know he anxieties about vocational choice and the power which is released when a real resolution of this problem is made. It will be worth the teacher's effort to make some systematic study of the various attempts to analyze the life of the adolescent in terms of the developmental tasks he faces. Most of these tasks, though they have a biological root, are to be defined primarily in relation to the demands of society upon the maturing adolescent. There is, however, a deeper dimension in the understanding of the student which is equally or more significant for the teacher.

This deeper dimension has to do more with the interior life of the student, though it obviously affects his external adjustments and his ways of meeting the cultural demands. The persistent problem of the adolescent so far as the internal structure and dynamics of his personality have been understood is that of achieving a sense of self-identity and of avoiding identity diffusion. Something has already been said of this. It not only is of focal significance for each of the so-called developmental tasks which are culturally determined—for example, choosing a vocation, having new and more mature relations with age mates of both sexes, achieving emotional independence from one's parents, accepting one's physique, and so on—but it is the crucial focus for the development of mature selfhood. As the student moves toward the stage of early adulthood (and many of them will already have done so), his sense of identity may be well advanced. He now faces the strategic issue which Erik Erickson calls the "achievement of intimacy." It is only after a "reasonable sense of identity has been established that real *intimacy* with the other sex (or, for that matter with any other person or even with oneself) is possible." [4] Erickson is not just speaking of sexual intimacy. What he has in mind is "that late-adolescent need for a kind of fusion with the essence of other people." [5] The surer an individual becomes of himself (the more mature his sense of self-identity), the more he seeks his identity in and through interpersonal relations. When this is not accomplished in late adolescence or early adulthood out of his own resources, "he may either isolate himself and find, at best, highly stereotyped and formal interpersonal relations (formal in the sense of lacking in spontaneity, warmth, and real exchange of fellowship), or he must seek them in repeated attempts and repeated failures." [6] Such an understanding of what is going on inside the college student may not help the teacher to understand and work with individual students, but it may help him to understand the "existence situation" of the college student, the existence situation to which all effective learning in this period of life must be relevant.

Within such an understanding of the existence situation of the modern college student it may be possible to isolate types of student response to that situation. To be sure, typologies may be dangerous, for they oversimplify and may make us forget that the adolescent personality is in flux. Students are growing; they are experimenting with various roles. Their orientations change, yet there are doubtless characteristic ways in which different students may attempt to work their way through what is both their predicament and their opportunity. Not much is known in this area as yet. It may be that typologies of workers like Fromm or Horney can be adapted to help us understand the variety of responses in terms of character structure. Some studies like those of Charles Morris may be helpful.[7] Morris confronted student groups in various parts of the world with descriptions of more than a dozen "Ways to Live," descriptions of ways of living which were clearly distinguishable from one another. He asked them to rank the ways to live according to their personal preferences. Through factor analysis he was able to isolate and classify the elements in preferred patterns and to make a beginning at least in understanding the social, psychological, and biological determinants of the preferences. Or perhaps Roy Heath's analysis of his evidence in the Princeton University study may be a beginning.[8] Heath constructs a personality model out of an identification of seven integrative personality types among his students. He characterizes his various types as the Reasonable Adventurer, the Middle of the Roader, the Hustler, the Politician, the Innovator, the Non-Committer, the Trapped, the Status Seeker, the Worrier, and the Over-Reactor. Heath's names alone are suggestive. Perhaps each of us could recognize among our students one or more of these types on the basis of the names themselves. We may have given enough thought to this problem to be able to indicate ways in which teaching can be most effective with respect to one or another of these types of students.

The emphasis of our thinking so far has been necessary, I think. If we are to increase our effectiveness as Christian teachers through a more penetrating understanding of the existence situation of the college student, we ought to attend to those aspects of the situation which characterize the "normal" student: the common patterns of experience which all of them face. They will meet these tasks in characteristic ways, depending upon their resources and their basic personality orientations. Another way of coming to an understanding of the student is to try to grasp the meaning of the issues faced by the so-called problem student. This focus might lead some to think that students with problems are somehow abnormal. Quite the contrary is true. Even the majority of students treated by college mental hygiene departments are "normal boys and girls" who "react at times, according to the circumstances of their lives, in much the same way as those who are popularly considered 'abnormal.' " [9] They may have periods of anxiety and depression. They may be emotionally disturbed in other ways, but as a group they constitute a cross section of the college or university.

A study of student problems is then another way of coming at a discovery of what is going on inside the student. Clements C. Fry in his report on his experience in the Department of University Health at Yale gives an illuminating account of the kinds of problems the late adolescent faces within the context of college and university life.[10] Again many of the same characteristic difficulties are described: the relationship to family, the coming to terms with sexual growth and the problems of sex behavior, social adjustment, and particularly scholastic adjustment. The advantage of this kind of approach, once we reject the notion that having problems is a sign of abnormality, is that we can look at the ways in which the tensions and resources of the academic community affect the facing of typical adolescent problems. The problems of family, of sexual adjustment, of social adjustment are typical of adolescence in our culture, but the college setting provides a specialized context within which these problems have to be faced. Awareness of the typical problems faced by one's students both because they are adolescents and because they are adolescents *in college* may be an important clue to the teacher who would understand the world of the college student and his existence situation.

It would be easy to misunderstand what I am trying to say here. I am not maintaining that every teacher ought to reorganize his teaching (course content, and so on) so that he ministers directly to the students' interests, problems, developmental tasks. What I am saying is that the more sensitive the Christian teacher is to the total person of the learner, the more capable he will be of releasing the students' intellectual capacities. The more such teaching is available to the student, the more open he will become toward those factors which produce personal growth and maturity. Only then can he face the real option of the Christian faith as a way of responding, of becoming a center of love and freedom to other persons and to his world. The release of intellectual capacities and of the capacities to learn in the wider dimensions of the learning process (attitudes, personal orientation) is as relevant to the well-adjusted mature adolescent as it is to those who are having particular difficulties in one or another area of their lives. It is as relevant to the good student as to the mediocre student. It is as relevant to the mediocre student as to the failing student. To be sure, a teacher who understands the existence situation of the modern college student may make adjustments in his selection of course content, in his emphases, in the organization and the handling of his subject matter. This is all gain. But more than this, such understanding may make an important difference in the way in which he "handles his students."

All that I have been saying about the importance of understanding the student mind, the existence situation, types of students, is even more appropriately said about understanding the individual student when the teacher works with him as an individual. The decisive thing here is to understand enough about the given individual to help him to make the most of his learning abilities. The teacher's task is to facilitate the student's learning. To do this he must know enough about students and about this particular student to discover what stands in the way of the student's learning, what keeps him from releasing his greatest powers. Much of what needs to be said in this matter needs also to be said within the context of a discussion of the Christian teacher's responsibility as counselor.

So far we have been interested in understanding the student as student, as late adolescent, facing the hopes and fears of his generation, immersed in the context of college or university life, with the experiences of stress and the resources for growth which are characteristic of such communities. It is important to look at the student from this perspective, to see the sociocultural situation out of which he comes, and to be sensitive to the wider range of forces which

continue to affect his concerns and needs through their influence on the educational community of which he is a part.
It is important also to have some insight into the stresses
and opportunities of late adolescence experienced in the
academic community. The college or university student is
also, however, a representative man, and it is of great consequence that the Christian teacher should have a depth
understanding of human nature itself as a context for com-
prehending the unique and the typical in the life of his students. Many areas of study can contribute to such a depth
understanding. Both the sciences of man and Christian
theology provide insights into the nature of man which
illuminate not only the life of the student but that of the
teacher himself, quite as much as they may serve as interpretative guides to the understanding of men and women in
other walks of life. Most fruitful perhaps of the sciences of
man is dynamic psychology. The recognition, for example,
of the extent to which our feelings and behavior are produced by forces beyond the reach of normal conscious awareness, or the detailed accounts of the defense mechanisms
each of us uses to reduce the stress of anxiety, or the emphasis on the significance of childhood experience in forming
character structure, to cite just three such insights, illus-
trates one important kind of contribution to self-understanding and to the understanding of those with whom we
work.

Christian theology provides another kind of perspective
and insight. It represents the interpretation of man's life
from the perspective of his relationship to God. Here is the
Christian teacher's key to both the dignity and the misery
of man, to both the potentiality and the threat to the fulfillment of the college and university student. The student's

freedom, his developing selfhood, his anxiety, sense of guilt, his creativeness, his responsiveness to love, his need for both judgment and forgiveness, are all put within the context of God's relationship to the individual and to the historical human communities. The Christian notions of man as creature, of the image of God in man and man's sin, together with the doctrines of God's judgment and his forgiveness, provide both an interpretative guide and a directive for Christian action. Teachers not only have much to learn from Christian doctrines of man about themselves and about their students, but they have much to contribute toward the criticism, the interpretation, and the reconstruction of such doctrines. The testing place of the adequacy of the formulation of Christian doctrine lies in the concrete experience of persons and relationships. The teaching-learning process is one such area of concrete experience in which such testing can take place and from which new insights into the meaning of the Christian faith can arise.

Chapter IX

THE CHRISTIAN TEACHER
AS COUNSELOR

I HAVE BEEN SPEAKING ABOUT THE IMPORTANCE OF UNDERSTAND-
ing the student mind, the existence situation of the contemporary college student. I have also mentioned the desira-
bility of understanding the individual student and expressed
the belief that these two kinds of understanding are mutually enriching. My intention was to describe some of the ways
in which we can increase our knowledge of the student,
since I am convinced that such a background of knowledge
makes it possible for us to be more effective teachers.
Whether we make the most of this possibility is another
matter. Knowledge alone will not do it for us, but it may
provide the ground for a kind of unconscious rapport and
sensitivity to the student on our part.

Whether or not our jobs are so defined as to include a
responsibility for counseling students, sooner or later students will come to us with their problems. Some of these
problems will have arisen in connection with their academic
work, but many of them will represent other areas of the
student's life: his vocational plans, his relations to his fel-

low students, to other teachers, to family. The longer we work with students, the more we will find, I think, that there is no clear separation. Difficulty in one area of a student's life will affect the other areas. Anxiety arising out of the student's relationship to his parents or to his fellow students may play havoc with his academic progress. We are also likely to discover that the initial representation of a problem may on examination prove to be a facade for the real difficulty. This may be a surprise to the student as well as to the teacher. What seems to be a purely academic problem, for example, inability to study effectively or failure in some particular subject, may turn out to be only a symptom of a different kind of difficulty in some other area of the student's life.

Most of us, I suppose, have not given a great deal of thought to this matter of counseling students. We think of ourselves primarily as teachers within a given discipline. We accept the task of counseling students, if at all, as a minor part of our job. Some of us enjoy these more intimate and informal relationships with students. Others may resent the amount of time and effort which such demands take from other activities in which we are more interested. My own judgment is that we need to give careful consideration to the basis for the teacher's role as a counselor both from the standpoint of education and from that of the Christian faith. Beyond whatever sense of responsibility such a consideration creates, each teacher ought to look at his own feelings in the matter and at his own effectiveness as a counselor. Whatever our sense of responsibility, I do not think anything is gained in trying to hold every teacher to the expansion of his teaching role in the direction of more counseling. Certainly if he resents this part of his work or is ineffective in it, he may do the students more harm than good. In addition he may be limiting his effectiveness in other areas where he could be doing a better job.

Having expressed such an opinion, I believe it must also be said that the counseling role is itself both an educational role and a means through which a teacher can express his sense of Christian vocation in a unique way. Counseling is itself a kind of indirect form of education. It is a way of fostering the growth and maturity of the individual in many areas of his life. It may further be directly related to academic achievement in its narrower sense. I have tried to indicate previously how closely learning is tied to the other areas of a student's life, to his anxiety, to his fear, his emotional maturity or immaturity. What is seen again and again in the failing student—that failure is not always a reflection of low intellectual capacity—can be seen also in the more "normal" student who seems not to learn at full capacity. Recent evidence reported from two institutions helps to substantiate this assertion of the interpenetration of the academic and the other areas of student life.

At one college each of the students on academic probation was assigned to one of the new teaching fellows under a Ford Foundation grant. These teaching fellows were beginning teachers. They had no professional training as counselors. They were simply asked to be "friends" to their counselees. It was suggested that they go out of their way to show interest in the particular students assigned to them, to be ready to talk over student problems, to be "available" to them. At the end of the school year a study disclosed a marked increase in the proportion of these probationary students who "got off pro" in comparison with the experience of previous years. Such an example can be only an illustration. It was not a controlled experiment. Causal factors are impossible to establish or isolate. It does, however, tend to support what many teachers have found from their own experience—that a counseling relationship may help to release powers in the student which he had previously been unable to use.

Another example reported from a large university helps to establish the same point. At this university a special study was being made of the nature of the four-year undergraduate experience as seen and felt by the undergraduate himself. A group of "normal" undergraduates was selected and a control group established. The first group was interviewed regularly and at some depth over a period of four years by a clinical psychologist. The purpose of these interviews was not to be therapeutic. They were an attempt to get resources to describe the factors and conditions in the university situation which affected the life and progress of undergraduates. The psychologist reports, however, that a very large proportion of these interview situations eventually did become therapeutic, and this on the initiative of the students. He also reports that a study of this group at the end of the four-year period as compared with the control group showed a higher level of academic achievement in the former group. Release for higher academic achievement seems to have been a by-product of this sustained interpersonal relationship in which problems could be talked out and experiences shared.

For the teacher who is interested in and capable of working with students at this close level, the counseling role is defensible both in relation to general educational goals and in relation to specific subject-matter learning.

Counseling students is not extraneous to their education. Nor need it be regarded as coddling on the one hand nor simply a matter for the professional counselor on the other.

There is a further and very important consideration for the Christian teacher. If the vocation of a Christian teacher is to be understood within the larger framework which I sketched earlier, then he may see his role as a counselor as a very serious part of his own Christian vocation. My contention was, you may remember, that the Christian teacher is not a propagandist or an apologist for the Christian faith. Rather, as a Christian he will seek to demonstrate the meaning of the gospel in relation to all that he does: in what he is as a person, in the way in which he handles his subject matter, in the way in which he relates to students, in his own self-understanding. His whole life, including his formal teaching, may be regarded as a kind of ministry to persons. He is an instrument for the reclamation of the human situation, the renewing of life, the redemption of the tragic character of existence, the mutual ministry of reconciliation to all men. Nowhere else perhaps in his role as teacher is it possible for him to express so directly in action his sense of the meaning of the Christian life. To be sure, some kinds of student problems may be overly dignified by relating them to such a conception of Christian vocation, but even with these his actions may symbolize and communicate much more than appears on the surface. A cup of cold water may on occasion mean much more than an apparently great act of deliverance on another.

Having stated a case for the Christian teacher as counselor, I believe it must be kept fully in mind that the teacher is not a professional counselor and that counseling is not his major responsibility. Nor should my interpretation of the teacher's role as counselor be taken to imply condemnation of those Christian teachers whose differing talents, interests, or other responsibilities prevent them from assuming such a role. Each of us must choose where he can do his best work and what his role is to be. For those whose opportunities for counseling and interest in counseling are great, an acquaintance with some of the general principles of effective counseling will be desirable. Some of these we pick up from experience, some from reading. All of us might profit by an inservice program of training or at least by discussion with our colleagues and with whatever professional counseling staff our college or university may afford.

More important than particular techniques or specialized training for the teacher-counselor is the matter of basic attitude and what might be called a philosophy of working with students. Good counseling is aimed at helping the student to achieve greater self-understanding, to make a realistic appraisal of his own problems. Sometimes it may be a matter of helping a student to find ways of tolerating a difficult situation for which there is no present solution. A teacher must try to create the kind of atmosphere in which a student will be willing to open up. He must be willing to take the time to be sure that the problem which the student feels or with which he initiates discussion is what is really bothering him. Oftentimes it is a device, and the student is waiting to see if he dare open up on something quite different. Sometimes the student himself mistakes the cause of his difficulty. Directive advice, forthright diagnosis, coldness, unapproachability, a judgmental attitude, tend to create defensiveness and foreclose many of the potentialities in a counseling situation. Readiness to listen, willingness to see the problem from the student's perspective, an atmosphere of warmth and acceptance on the part of the teacher, help to provide the context in which a student will venture out, giving some expression to his real feelings. Not until this is done is it possible to help the student clarify his own understanding of these feelings or to work through his problem, utilizing the constructive resources that are latent in him. The ultimate goal is not only to help the student find his own solution to a particular problem, but to help him move to greater independence and freedom. The counselor needs to be careful, therefore, not to act in such a fashion as to increase the student's relation of dependence, unless he sees that this will ultimately issue in a growing capacity of the individual to manage his own affairs. The teacher who counsels a student is certainly not responsible for solving the student's problems for him, but he does have the task of helping the student to release the power latent in him for meeting these problems.

One way of summarizing what a good counselor may do is to say that he can try to create a relationship of trust in which the student can find a sufficient release from his anxieties, his negative feelings, his own doubts about himself and his own worth, to begin to work through these feelings with some insight and increasing resolution. Opening up to another person in a relationship of trust is often the most difficult part of the battle. Once this is done, the difficulties, the confusion, the inner conflict, may perhaps be talked through until some clarity emerges and the individual feels able to resolve his problem in terms of his new self-understanding or his increased comprehension of the issue facing him. Often, too, difficulties are unearthed which are more than the untrained counselor can handle or which necessitate a more sustained kind of help than a teacher can normally give. A teacher who takes his role as counselor seriously may be of great service to students and to the college in cases of this kind. He can see to it that such students get the professional help they require. The number of students who need this kind of help is by no means small. Experts on the mental health problems of college students estimate that 10 to 15 per cent of a student body need the resources that a psychiatrical service provides. Probably the number is larger if we include those students who could profit by a sustained relationship to a professionally trained college counselor. Colleges, of course, are not hospitals, but unless they can in their selection procedures eliminate from the college population the emotionally unstable and those who are particularly vulnerable to the stress of college life, they have some obligation for helping those who are not so seriously disturbed as to be excluded from the college community.

A college teacher ought to be able to recognize the signs in a student which indicate that professional help is needed. The Committee on the College Student of the Group for the Advancement of Psychiatry suggests some of these:

persistent anxiety states where the cause is not clear, bodily symptoms, mild mood swings, sleeplessness, panic in examinations, and errors in judgment exemplified by the student who attempts to do more work than he can accomplish successfully.

The report then adds:

Finally, there are some very serious symptoms that always call for referral without delay to the physician or psychiatrist. These include bizarre behavior that "just doesn't make sense," over-activity with excitement and increased irritability, exhibitionism, suicidal threats or acts, homicidal threats, acts indicative of extreme hostility, or any persistent form of behavior that indicates a deep degree of emotional instability.[1]

Such students are obviously a minority. Even those who might profit by a sustained professional counseling relationship are a minority of the student population. The greater number of students are wrestling with difficulties caused by their movement through adolescence, complicated by the specific tensions created by the academic environment in the midst of a total world in which insecurity, anxiety, and stress of various kinds affect us all. This process is fraught with difficulty for many. As one of the characters in Marcel's plays says: "There is only one suffering, to be alone." It is a part of the ministry of the Christian teacher to his students to see to it that they are spared at least a part of this suffering—that they are not alone.

Chapter X

THE CHRISTIAN TEACHER AND THE COLLEGE COMMUNITY

THE CHRISTIAN TEACHER FACES ANOTHER PROBLEM NOT unlike that which confronts him when he is called upon to counsel the individual student. Sooner or later, particularly if we have taught in a number of different kinds of colleges or universities, we become acutely aware of the larger context in which our teaching activities are carried on. I have already mentioned some of the factors operative in the student's growth and learning from the larger cultural context. The influence of class and social background and the corresponding expectations and demands of both students and parents are such factors. Obviously there are many others. The student brings with him characteristic attitudes of a political, economic, and cultural origin which affect his learning and his growth as a person. Contemporary changes and disturbances in the larger society impinge upon his life, affecting his stability, his sense of security, his motivations, and his values. All of us are aware, for example, of the effects of the outbreak of the Second World War on the student mind. Teachers can be more or less sensitive to these factors which affect all of our lives as we study and teach. Neither teacher nor student lives in a vacuum. A teacher who has begun to think through his own philosophy of education not only will be aware of the impact of these influences on his teaching and on his students, but he will probably have some view embracing the hopes he may have for the possible reciprocal influence of education on this larger culture.

True as all this may be, the life of the student and the teacher, and so the teaching-learning process, has its setting within a more immediate cultural context whose pervasive influence upon that process may be even more decisive. In more than one sense the college or university is a culture or a subculture in its own right. It has its own life style, its characteristic patterns of interaction, its own history and traditions. It is a complex whole, possessing distinctive ways of feeling, valuing, and acting. This web of influences provides the pervasive quality of college or university life. It conditions positively or negatively every learning experience both in the narrower academic sense and in the larger sense of movement toward personal maturity. In varying degrees the personality of student, teacher, and administrator are shaped in this culture and by this culture. In varying degrees through social or individual influence they in turn shape its form and spirit. Within the framework of a particular college or university culture it is possible to isolate the structure and dynamics of the life of the community. Doubtless it would be helpful if some sociologist or cultural anthropologist could turn the light of his discipline with its tools of analysis and its modes of conceptualization upon our particular college communities. We might then see more clearly the interrelationships of one element to another and of the whole to its parts. We might better be able to assess the impact of these influences on educational achievement. Perhaps we could locate within the scene the factors which facilitate learning and those which make it more difficult, those which increase the student's maturity and those which perpetuate immature patterns of behavior and learning.

In the absence of any such systematic and careful analyses the Christian teacher will have to approach this area of understanding in his own way. As laymen in social analysis we may want to look at our own particular college or university community and appraise the impact of its way of life and of the various elements within its structure and functioning upon the total learning experience of our students. Increased understanding alone may be helpful, for as we know better the characteristic tensions, problems, and resources of student life on our campus, we may be able to be more effective in our teaching and in our relationships to students. Probably no single teacher can do more than this by his own efforts. He would be an unusual person who could bring about any large change in the cultural pattern of his college community by himself. The whole faculty, however, or a group within the faculty could over a period of time, self-consciously and with forethought, have a very significant impact on the patterning of life within the college or university. Understanding one's college community in some depth is the first step toward its guided transformation. A Christian teacher or a group of such teachers may well assist in the realistic appraisal of the existing situation and the assessment of its possibilities.

What I am writing about has to do only in part with what are ordinarily called "extracurricular activities." It is much more than this. It is the total configuration of student life and perhaps of faculty life and attitude as well. It includes the college-sponsored extracurricular activities, but it also includes the pattern of custom, behavior, and attitude which shapes the mind of the incoming student and to some extent at least binds the lives of all the members of the college community.

There are colleges where the intellectual life is taken with great seriousness; there are other colleges where study and thought seem to be merely the external justification for athletics and for having a good time. There are institutions in which the life of the mind is carried on with little relevance to the ultimate questions confronting man or to the great issues facing society. There are others in which relevance to such questions is explicit and ever-present for both students and faculty. These are matters of what the anthropologist Herskovits calls "cultural focus." We need as Christian teachers to know what determines the "cultural focus" of our particular institution, how this focus is related to our educational goals, and how it can be changed if that is necessary.

Not only is it important to understand the cultural focus of a college community, but it is also of great potential import for one's teaching and work with students to comprehend the structure and dynamics of student life. The central issue is not the understanding in itself but the sensing of the relationship between these factors and the maturity and learning of the students. Most of us working in a college or university are aware of the power groups in the student culture. We may not go much further. What we need to ask is what determines role and status? What influences the quality of interpersonal and intergroup relationships on our college campus? How do such factors condition learning and the movement of the student toward maturity? Most of us who know individual students to any degree at all are aware of the influence of the external surroundings and the material difficulties of student life on students—on both their learning and the emerging quality of their lives. We know that students who work long hours in self-support or that those who commute face problems which other students do not have to meet. Let me quickly add, lest I be misunderstood, that I am not proposing the elimination of problems or difficulties in the lives of students. What is needed, however, is an awareness of the nature of the stress-producing factors in student life and of the many resources for growth and fulfillment in the college community. If some aspects of student life are unhealthy from the point of view of movement toward maturity, if they inhibit rather than facilitate learning, we should be cognizant of these facts and take what steps we can to alter the circumstances. If other elements in the campus social structure are resources for growth toward mature living and learning, these too should be recognized and used as effectively as possible.

Let me be more specific: If the character of fraternity-sorority life, the emphasis on athletics, the existing structure of student government, the lack of opportunity for mature relationships between the sexes, are unhealthy influences in the college community, the Christian teacher will want to be aware of such facts. He will want to work with others to eliminate or transform these unhealthy influences in order to make the context for the educational task as productive as possible.

On the other hand, it may be that the teacher will see

gaps in student experience which need to be filled. Perhaps the college community is relatively isolated and its cultural life impoverished, perhaps most of its students come from families whose social and economic resources have limited their acquaintance with the richness of the cultural heritage in arts and literature, or perhaps they have come from such privileged homes or schools that they have never confronted the depths of human need to be discovered in blighted areas, among the aged, the mentally ill, or even the poor in their own community. It may be that opportunity for association with faculty outside the classroom is what is needed. Perhaps a professional counseling service is required, or one may find that the churches in the local community are unable to minister effectively to the religious concerns of students. They may not have the personnel; they may not understand the student's needs; they may be unable to translate the gospel in such a fashion that students can keep both their intellectual integrity and their religious commitment. A Christian teacher who is aware of such needs may with his colleagues help to find ways of meeting them.

What any teacher can do in these matters will vary greatly with each situation. Obviously the small college presents a very different set of possibilities than the large university. The teacher's conception of his own role, his status, and his interests will make a difference. The kind of administration and the quality of administrative faculty relationship, the relation of the college to its larger local community, to its own history and tradition, to its alumni— these all introduce variables which make generalization difficult. My point is, however, a simple one. What we need to be continually aware of as Christian teachers is the constant educative influence of the larger context in which our teaching is set. Again and again we find those who claim that the "value of education is due to college life even more than to college instruction" [1] or who, like Whitehead, point to the fact that much of the richness and breadth of our educational experience comes from what takes place apart from the lecture room and its formal studies. For Whitehead it was education through "incessant conversation" with friends, undergraduates, or members of the staff. He writes of these conversations:

This started with dinner at about six or seven, and went on till about ten o'clock in the evening, stopping sometimes earlier and sometimes later. In my own case, there would then follow two or three hours' work at mathematics. . . . We discussed everything—politics, religion, philosophy, literature—with a bias toward literature. . . . Looking backwards across more than half a century, the conversations have the appearance of a daily Platonic dialogue.[2]

Not all students have such a profitable experience outside the lecture room. The life in many colleges and universities fosters immaturity, negates and thwarts effective learning, and creates habits of thought and feeling as well as situations of stress and tension which are not conducive to either academic learning or growth toward maturity. It is my conviction that the Christian teacher who understands something of the structure, the dynamics, and the pervasive culture of a college or university community will better understand the student. He will know more clearly both what is shaping the student's mind and behavior and what is creating problems for him. Understanding the individual and the general climate of student life may make more effective teaching possible in the classroom. It will, moreover, provide the ground for any intelligent attempt to transform the life of the college community or to introduce new elements into the situation in such a way as to foster both the student's learning and his maturity.

Chapter XI

GOD AND THE
TEACHING-LEARNING PROCESS

WE HAVE BEEN NOTING WHAT IT MEANS TO BE A CHRISTIAN teacher. I have indicated some of the Christian teacher's concerns in higher education and have pointed to some of the differences it may make to one's teaching if he takes the Christian faith seriously. The suggestion has been made that to be a Christian teacher is to have a sense of calling, to look upon one's role as teacher as a religious vocation, as a ministry within and through a particular kind of professional activity. Such a conception of his work will affect the way in which the teacher handles his subject matter and his method of teaching. It will influence his interest in and relationship to his students both within and outside the classroom. It will make a difference in his role in the larger community. Some of these differences have been described. In many respects, however, the good Christian teacher will not be different from the good secular teacher. Good teaching has certain common characteristics no matter who the teacher or what his ultimate loyalty. There will be still other instances in which both the Christian teacher and the secular teacher may seem to be doing the same things, and yet there may be important differences between them. I have already indicated that behind similar behavior patterns there may be essential differences of understanding, experience, and motivation. Two teachers may teach in much the same way, yet their understanding of what they are trying to do and their motivation for doing it may be conspicuously different. Just as two men may marry and marry for different reasons, with differing goals and differing understandings of the meaning of the marriage relationship, so the identity of observable processes in teaching or any other area does not ensure an identity of meaning.

What is true of motivation, goal, and self-understanding with respect to the teacher's role is also true when it comes to interpreting the meaning of the teaching-learning process as a whole. Confronted by the same phenomena, the Christian teacher will see its meaning within the total context of the Christian understanding of life, while the non-Christian will interpret it in some other fashion. This is one of the most important distinctions between the Christian teacher and the non-Christian teacher. The one will interpret not only his own role but the whole teaching-learning process by means of the categories of the Christian faith. The other will not. As a Christian a teacher has come to have a certain kind of understanding of how God discloses himself in the human situation. He knows that God is not limited in his activity to what happens in churches or in the lives of individual Christians. God has not abandoned the world of nature or the world of man. He is not irrelevant to social, cultural, or interpersonal processes. He is active creatively and redemptively in and through all human experience. God is present in so-called secular existence as well as in what men call the sacred. When men realize this, there emerges in them a sense of the holy which is not limited to traditional religious associations. This sense is a counterpart of the feeling of duty and reverence held by Whitehead to be the essence of education, when he declared that the "essence of education is that it be religious." [1] I think that many teachers, at times at least, have this feeling toward their involvement in the educational process. However vaguely conceptualized or however dimly felt, many of us have a sense that something extraordinarily important goes on in the teaching-learning process. There is mystery here too. One might point to a kind of analogy between the work of the teacher and that of the farmer. There is a sowing, a cultivation, and a harvest. A good deal of the seed does not seem to take root; the increase is not of our own making, and for us at least much of the harvest is unseen. Or we might compare the teacher's art to the physician's. Just as the physician prescribes the diet, alters the conditions of life by advising rest, change of scene or climate, and administers medicines which help the body fight off its sickness, so the teacher prescribes the intellectual diet of his students, modifies the context for learning, and gives support through word and feeling in order to facilitate the learning of his students or to provide conditions under which students with one kind of difficulty or another can overcome them. Yet the healing whether of mind or body is not solely due to the physician or to the patient. No more so is the emergence of new understanding or the overcoming of difficulties in learning to be attributed solely either to the teacher or to his students. Something more is involved in both cases. What we sense is that in the complex interaction of influences and events some kind of creative order-ing and transforming process is going on beyond man's control and often beyond his intent. When one becomes vividly aware of this as he sees some striking example of emergent meaning or creative transformation, he may be moved to awe and wonder. Yet perhaps most striking of all is the quiet presence of this creative ordering and trans-forming process through the whole of teaching and learn-ing. It is there at least for those who have the eyes to see.

My point is that the Christian teacher has eyes to see. He also has the conceptual framework within which to interpret this deeper meaning of the teaching-learning process which many only dimly feel and others miss entirely. The interpretation of the religious meaning of the teaching-learning process should, I suppose, be the task of the pro-fessional theologian. Not many theologians have, however, addressed this problem. Only two classic attempts to give a theological interpretation of the teaching-learning process come to mind, namely, those of Augustine and Thomas Aquinas. Augustine's dialogue on teaching is centered in the epistemological problem. He is interested in how knowl-edge of the truth is attained, how ideas are communicated, what part teaching plays in the process of learning. His answer is that the human teacher only elicits the truth. Truth is not taught by man. All truth comes from God, whose eternal truth, Christ, is man's inward teacher. There is no teacher finally who teaches man knowledge except God through Christ.[2] In principle Thomas Aquinas agrees with Augustine. Using Aristotle's distinction between active and passive potency, he is able to distinguish more precisely the function of the human teacher and God, the ultimate teacher.[3]

The Christian teacher and the Christian theologian may finally come to agree with both Augustine and Aquinas, though they may prefer to state the position somewhat differently. Yet neither of these classic theologians is of very much help in interpreting the breadth and depth of what we have come to discuss as the teaching-learning process. If, as I have suggested, the Christian teacher is to view the process as a whole within a Christian framework, he will need to make a different initial approach and will have to look directly again at specific examples of the teaching-learning process. Let us consider carefully an account of a teaching-learning situation. The illustration is from the well-known autobiography of Helen Keller. Miss Keller writes of her first experience with her famous teacher, Anne Mansfield Sullivan:

The morning after my teacher came she led me into her room and gave me a doll. The little blind children at the Perkins Institution had sent it and Laura Bridgman had dressed it; but I did not know this until afterward. When I had played with it a little while, Miss Sullivan slowly spelled into my hand the word "d-o-l-l." I was at once interested in this finger play and tried to imitate it. When I finally succeeded in making the letters correctly I was flushed with childish pleasure and pride. . . . I did not know that I was spelling a word or even that words existed; I was simply making my fingers go in monkey-like imitation. In the days that followed I learned to spell in this uncomprehending way a great many words, among them *pin, hat, cup* and a few verbs like *sit, stand and walk*. But my teacher had been with me several weeks before I understood that everything has a name. . . .

We walked down the path to the well-house, attracted by the fragrance of the honeysuckle with which it was covered. Some one was drawing water and my teacher placed my hand under the spout. As the cool stream gushed over one hand she spelled into the other hand the word *water*, first slowly, then rapidly. I stood still, my whole attention fixed upon the motions of her fingers. Suddenly I felt a misty consciousness as of something forgotten—a thrill of returning thought; and somehow the mystery of language was revealed to me. I knew that "w-a-t-e-r" meant the wonderful cool something that was flowing over my hand. That living word awakened my soul, gave it light, hope, joy, set it free! There were barriers still, it is true, but barriers that could in time be swept away.

I left the well-house eager to learn. Everything had a name, and each name gave birth to a new thought. As we returned to the house every object which I touched seemed to quiver with life. That was because I saw everything with the strange, new sight that had come to me.

I remember the morning that I first asked the meaning of the word, "love." This was before I knew many words. I had found a few early violets in the garden and brought them to my teacher. She tried to kiss me; but at that time I did not like to have any one kiss me except my mother. Miss Sullivan put her arm gently round me and spelled into my hand, "I love Helen."

"What is love?" I asked.

She drew me closer to her and said, "It is here," pointing to my heart, whose beats I was conscious of for the first time. Her words puzzled me very much because I did not then understand anything unless I touched it.

I smelt the violets in her hand and asked, half in words, half in signs, a question which meant, "Is love the sweetness of the flowers?"

"No," said my teacher.

Again I thought. The warm sun was shining upon us.

"Is this not love?" I asked, pointing in the direction from which the heat came, "Is this not love?"

It seemed to me that there could be nothing more beautiful

than the sun, whose warmth makes all things grow. But Miss Sullivan shook her head, and I was greatly puzzled and disappointed. I thought it strange that my teacher could not show me love.

A day or two afterward I was stringing beads of different sizes in symmetrical groups—two large beads, three small ones, and so on. I had made many mistakes, and Miss Sullivan had pointed them out again and again with gentle patience. Finally I noticed a very obvious error in the sequence and for an instant I concentrated my attention on the lesson and tried to think how I should have arranged the beads. Miss Sullivan touched my forehead and spelled with decided emphasis, "Think."

In a flash I knew that the word was the name of the process that was going on in my head. This was my first conscious perception of an abstract idea. For a long time I was still—I was not thinking of the beads in my lap, but trying to find a meaning for "love" in the light of this new idea. The sun had been under a cloud all day, and there had been brief showers; but suddenly the sun broke forth in all its southern splendor.

Again I asked my teacher, "Is this not love?"

"Love is something like the clouds that were in the sky before the sun came out," she replied. Then in simpler words than these, which at that time I could not have understood, she explained: "You cannot touch the clouds, you know; but you feel the rain and know how glad the flowers and the thirsty earth are to have it after a hot day. You cannot touch love either; but you feel the sweetness that it pours into everything. Without love you would not be happy or want to play."

The beautiful truth burst upon my mind—I felt that there were invisible lines stretched between my spirit and the spirits of others.[4]

This illustration from Helen Keller's experience might be a paradigm for much human learning. It could be analyzed for the psychological dynamics which are involved.

It could be studied in relation to learning theory or contemporary theories of communication. No such approach would of itself answer the kind of question which concerns us: What is the significance of what is happening in this teaching-learning situation? What one sees going on here is the emergence of meaning. One kind of experience (doll) is being connected with another kind of experience (an abstraction—a spelled word) so that the one experience can stand for the other in such a way that the two experiences enrich each other. Here in Miss Keller's account there is depicted the growth of mind and feeling through creative intercommunication. New insights, new feelings, new qualities of experience, are emerging out of the old. All are being woven together in a web of interconnectedness so that they are mutually enriching and mutually supporting. Yet one cannot say that either Miss Sullivan or Helen Keller had control of the process by which these emergent meanings came into being. Something of what I have tried to point to in Helen Keller's first meeting with Miss Sullivan is what the Christian theologian would mean by the creative activity of God. Henry Nelson Wieman has attempted to describe how God acts in and through the structures of human experience. He writes:

A process of reorganization is going on, generating new meanings, integrating them with the old, endowing each event as it occurs with a wide range of reference, molding the life of a man into a more deeply unified totality of meaning. The wide diversities, varieties, and contrasts of all the parts of a man's life are being progressively transformed into a more richly inclusive whole. The several parts of life are connected in mutual support, vivifying and enhancing one another in the creation of a more inclusive unity of events and possibilities.[5]

It is this process which creates and transforms human personality. It builds cultures and societies. It is God's way of working through interpersonal and intergroup relationships to bring to birth new good. It is one key to understanding the significance of what is taking place in the teaching-learning process. God is present and active in the teaching-learning process even when the teacher himself is unaware of his presence and has no sense of the religious meaning of his calling.

Such a theistic interpretation is only the beginning of getting at the religious depth of the teaching-learning process. As all teachers know, there are difficulties encountered along the way in one's teaching and in the students' learning. There is resistance in the students and in the situation. Some students have trouble learning; some don't want to learn. Some are unattractive to us personally. Many are difficult to understand. Judgment is an important part of the learning situation, and it is hard for the teacher to be fair in judging and hard for students to accept judgment. The Christian teacher should not have misgivings about the need for judgment because of Jesus' injunction "Judge not, that ye be not judged." That injunction was hardly meant to encourage either moral neutrality or refusal to evaluate work and attitudes critically. It appears rather to refer to the spirit in which one judges, condemning the censorious spirit and the self-righteousness which cut off relationship and destroy trust. The teacher himself will be judged, not only by his students and colleagues, but by his own internalized standards of excellence. He will experience judgment through his perception of his own inadequacies and through the comprehension of his failure in the teaching-learning process. Not only do judgment and acceptance in spite of judgment enter the teaching situation, but the teacher's own limitations, his pride, his anxiety, his sense of guilt, as well as his love, his devotion and his creativity are continually present. Can all this be understood in religious terms? All of these experiences are the very stuff of the Christian faith. They are universal human experiences. They are what the Christian faith is all about. Let us take just one example: the problem of acceptance. We know from our own experience that one of the keys to understanding the failure of communication lies in the phenomenon of rejection. The teacher who won't listen to the student's ideas, who is insensitive to the student's feelings and concerns, or who, worse still, seems to the student to have rejected him as a person has lost the battle of learning. Some students are easy to accept, but there are others, and these are the ones who most need acceptance. They are the difficult ones. If in the face of this kind of situation the teacher can give his students the certainty that they are accepted in spite of all that seems unacceptable about them, a new quality can enter into the teaching-learning process. This new quality is what Paul Tillich points to as the essence of true education. Such acceptance is an expression of agape—creative love—and true education is the expression of creative love. Following the Johannine tradition, Tillich finds the love of the Creator in all such love. Whoever participates in this love participates in God, and only in so far as one does participate in this love does he participate in God, "for agape is so much the innermost nature of God that God himself can be called Love." "Agape is the universal, unconditioned power of the creative life." [6] Of all human relationships the educative relationship is the one which should be creative, and true education is the expression of this creative love.

Yet agape is not without judgment. It is not sentimental. It judges in a realistic, nonsentimental way. A student, of course, may identify the judgment with the will of the teacher and feel rejected. The teacher then feels frustrated and attacked. An authoritarian teacher would try to break the resistance of the student, to suppress doubt or disobedience. A so-called progressive teacher, at least as Tillich understands him, would let the student go his own way. Both are wrong. In the first case, what is best in the human being (his creative love) is surrendered; in the second, emptiness and an unhappy liberty in which creative love is "without object and direction" are the result.[7] In contrast education filled with agape continues to accept the student. And, says Tillich, if the student feels accepted, he might also accept the teacher. The true teacher is the one who makes the student accept him, after he accepts the student. "A community which has grown in this way is a triumph of creative love and is the aim of all education."[8] To participate in education of this kind is to participate in the very life of God.

A vivid example of both the lack and the great need for this kind of acceptance within the teaching-learning situation is the following account drawn from a case report of a twelve-year-old boy written by his teacher:

Roger is twelve years old, almost three years older than any other child in the class. He has failed three different terms in school and was passed into the 6th grade this year only because of his age. Achievement and other tests at the end of the year showed little improvement over what he accomplished on the tests given in September. He has had psychological tests three times:

Once when he was 7, again when he was 9, and once more this spring. Test results showed that he has normal intelligence and is abnormal in no way. He has never learned to read although there is no physical or mental obstruction to his ability to learn. He is far beyond the average child in his ability to converse and shows remarkable common sense and judgment for a child his age. He surpasses most of the class in reasoning out classroom problems not connected with schoolwork. He has a wonderful personality and is well liked by all the other children although the boys call him a sissy. Roger firmly believes that he was born without a brain and that it is impossible for him to learn. He will not attempt to do any kind of school work which involves independent thinking and constantly attempts to foresee any challenge which might confront him before the school day even begins. Upon arriving at school he might say, "If we do examples at the board today I'm not going up. I'll sit in my seat beacuse I can't do them and only take up space at the board."

When Roger started to read in the first grade, the children laughed when he made a mistake and continued to laugh at his mistakes when none of his teachers corrected the other children. This occurred in more than the first grade. Roger at first laughed with them until he suddenly refused to read aloud any more. Since then he cannot even read silently. He dislikes school and has to be practically forced to school every day.[9]

What Roger apparently missed early in his school career was an atmosphere of acceptance, of creative love, which would bear with his difficulties and support him in working through them. It is just such acceptance which has been discovered to be one of the indispensable conditions for healing in that kind of re-education we call psychotherapy.

Can what I have been talking about, using illustrations from childhood, be seen clearly too at the different level of our own teaching, the teaching of college and university students? I think it can, and I should like to turn for my final illustration to Carl Becker's account of Frederick Jackson Turner as a teacher. Becker first heard of Turner from a lawyer in his home town before he left high school for the university. This man spoke highly of him as "Old Freddie Turner." Becker had asked what Turner taught. "Well, he teaches American history. But it's not what he teaches, the subject I mean. The subject doesn't matter. It's what he is, the personality and all that sort of thing. It's something he gives you, inspiration, new ideas, a fresh light on things in general. It's something he makes you want to do or be. I don't remember much American history, but I'll never forget that man Turner, old Freddie Turner." [10]

So Becker went to Wisconsin, and he took a course with Turner in history, since that was what Turner taught, though Becker regarded history as one of the dullest of academic subjects. Becker describes his early impression of Turner; his eyes, his manner, seemed to convey the attitude that the world was "full of a number of things that odd chances and interesting episodes were to be momentarily expected. Expected and welcomed." Such was the impression. Serious indeed the man was, you never doubted that, but not solemn, above all not old, not professionally finished; just beginning rather, zestfully and buoyantly beginning, out for adventure, up to something, in the most casual, friendly way inviting you to join in. [11]

Becker tells of his own difficulties with history. He took courses in history; he didn't study it—he didn't know how to study it. Then he says:

But if I didn't study history that year, I was infected with the desire to do so. This, of course, was Turner's fault, not mine. . . .

For it was true, as my lawyer friend said, that Turner had a singular capacity for making you want to do and be something—to do, in short, what he was doing, and to be, if possible, what he was. And what was he? And what was he doing? Fascinated by the man, I attended to his every gesture and expression, listened to everything he said, less at first for the content than for the voice, the intention, the implication. The implication of the whole performance was of something vital being under consideration, something that had in itself only incidentally to do with students "taking a course." The implication was that we (all of us together if *we* chose—that was our affair) were searching for something, ferreting out hidden secrets. Facts there were, plenty of them, and as a matter of course to be known: but that wasn't the end. There was something concealed there, in and behind the facts, some problem that concerned humanity at large waiting to be solved. The implication was that we might, on our own account, turn over the dead facts once more, on the chance of finding something, something the others had missed.[12]

Becker comments on Turner's method. "He didn't produce packets of useful information, no laying down of the law and gospel according to Turner." Rather, his lectures were "all compact of inquiry and novel ideas carelessly thrown out with more questions asked than were answered, more problems posed than solved." This did not bother Becker, for he says:

I was getting a great deal out of Turner. I was daily enjoying the inestimable privilege of watching an original and penetrating intelligence at work, playing freely with facts and ideas, handling with discrimination the problems of history, problems which so often turned out to be the problems of life itself. [One is reminded of an identical comment of Irwin Edman's on John Dewey's teaching] ... An ordered body of information I could get, and did afterwards get, for myself; but from no other man did I ever get in quite the same measure that sense of watching a first-class mind at work on its own account, and not merely rehearsing for the benefit of others; the most delightful sense in the world of sitting there waiting for ideas to be born; expectantly waiting for secret meanings, convenient explanatory hypotheses to be discovered, lurking as like as not under the dullest mass of drab facts ever seen.

In this happy way I got a new idea of history. It was after all no convention agreed upon to be learned by rote, but just the infinitely varied action and thought of men who in past times had lived and struggled and died for mean or great objects. It was in short an aspect of life itself, and as such something to be probed into, thought about, written about.[13]

Turner did not give answers to certain kinds of questions. "After I don't know how many months or years," says Becker, "I learned that the answers he commonly neglected to give were answers which would have enabled me to borrow his opinions and judgments and to save myself the trouble of thinking. He would do what he could to help me think, but he wouldn't if he knew it, tell me what to think."

On his relation to graduate students Becker writes:

To me at least it is a matter of no slight importance that he accepted us graduate students, in that spirit [of understanding]. We too were apparently parts of the universe, to be accepted as given. He never made me feel that I was before the Judgment Seat. He was never the schoolmaster, standing behind me prodding, with sharp exclamation points pitchforking me up to the steep path of learning. He criticized my work to be sure, but it was the work he criticized, and in the most honest friendly way, without leaving any aftertaste of personal depravity in the mouth. He appeared to take me as the associated fates had made me, more or less intelligent and to assume that I would willingly do the best I could. Amazing to me at least, was the casual friendly way he had of treating us as equals, as serious scholars with whom it was a pleasure to be associated in common tasks. Even our work he didn't criticize much, condemning it by silence mainly, commending it on rare occasions by a few hearty words of approval. How the rash man gambled on us to be sure, professing to see in us qualities and virtues marking us out for future savants. Perhaps there was some method in his madness. To get the best out of graduate students, or any students, it is perhaps just as well not to assume to begin with that there isn't any best to be got out.[14]

In this Turner illustration we can see all of the things we have already noted: the creativity at work—reorganizing, generating new meanings, integrating them with the old, molding Becker's life into a more deeply unified totality of meaning—Turner's acceptance and deep trust of his students, yet not without the element of judgment. Something else can be seen, something which Martin Buber has more than anyone else emphasized in his portrayal of the teaching process. Buber says that the essence of the educative process is communion. By this he means to point to that same quality in teaching which Tillich does when he talks about creative love, but he seems to me to give a fuller account of what is involved. Communion means "being opened up, and drawn in." It is what Buber calls "dialogue." Dialogue is a relationship between two persons in which there is "inclusion," "experiencing the other side." Two individuals share a common experience, but at least one of them "lives through the common event from the standpoint of the other." Dialogue is a relationship between an "I" and a "Thou," in which the person relates himself to the other in his full *personal* dimension rather than to the other as an object, an "It."

For Buber the teacher-student relationship is pure dialogue. The most inward achievement of this relation in education is trust. Because this teacher exists in this relation, meaninglessness is not all and cannot be the real truth. "Because this human being exists, in the darkness the light lies hidden, in fear salvation, and in the callousness of one's fellow men, the great Love." [15] This does not mean that the teacher must be perfect or as perfect as the student thinks he is, nor does it mean that he must maintain this dialogic relationship continually. But the teacher must be truly "there"; he must be truly "present." More than this, if the teacher has once gathered the student into his life, then there is a kind of subterranean dialogic—[16] a steady potential presence of the one to the other which endures. This is a new reality *between* them: mutuality.

Yet for Buber this teacher-student relationship is not one of pure inclusion, though it is based on inclusion. For unlike other forms of the dialogue, it is one-sided. The student is unable to enter fully into the teacher's world. If it loses its one-sidedness, it loses its essence. I think Buber is right, though perhaps as students become more mature, some of the onesidedness of the relationship is overcome. Education "means to let a selection of the world affect a person through the medium of another person." It is raising to a function and a law "what is otherwise found only as a grace inlaid in the folds of life": The teacher's calling is that of influencing "the being of other persons." [17]

The question of the norm or direction of education is a perplexing one in our time when the cultural or epochal norms are disintegrated and shattered. Buber writes: "When all the figures are shattered, when no figure is able any more to dominate and shape the present human material,'' [18] then it is clear that what must form and inform the teaching-learning process is the image of God. Thus the role of the teacher is defined. ''When all directions fail there arises in the darkness over the abyss the one true direction of man, towards the creative Spirit, towards the Spirit of God brooding on the face of the water, towards Him of whom we know not whence He comes and whither He goes.'' [19] The teaching-learning process becomes a process in which the teacher exposes himself and others to the creative Spirit. And the teacher can call upon the Creator to save and perfect his image. ''The ones who count are those persons who—though they may be of little renown—respond to and are responsible for the continuation of the living spirit, each in the active stillness of his sphere of work.'' [20]

Buber has given us a profound interpretation of the teaching process. I doubt very much that Frederick Jackson Turner would have used Buber's language to describe what was taking place in his relationships to his students. Probably Helen Keller and Ann Mansfield Sullivan, involved in a more intimate interpersonal relationship, would have come closer to his language. Yet both cases seem to me to be clear examples of Buber's conception of dialogue. Both teachers seem to have been profoundly able to ''experience the other side.'' In both cases there was the inward achievment of trust. Both teachers were ''there''; they were ''present.'' A kind of subterranean dialogic emerged, a presence of the one to the other which endured and undoubtedly continued to influence both Miss Keller and Carl Becker throughout their lives. In both cases there was the ''selection of the world'' affecting a ''person through the medium of another person.''

The religious meaning of Buber's dialogical interpretation of the teaching-learning process will not escape those who know his *I and Thou* and his other writings. For Buber, to enter into dialogue is to relate to the other as an I to a Thou, and every particular Thou is a glimpse through to the eternal Thou. In each Thou we address the eternal Thou.

Is God then present within the teaching-learning process? I believe that the Christian teacher will answer, "Yes." He will see God, the Creator and Redeemer, actively related to the whole of human existence including the sphere of education. Though it is difficult to separate the creative and redemptive working of God, certainly his creative activity will be seen in our dependence as man, and hence as teachers and students, upon God for the very possibility of our existence. God will be seen as the universal creative power which sustains all things including the educational process and those involved in it. God's creativeness will also be seen in the movement of human life toward the emergence of the new: new meanings, qualities, values, interrelationships, orders; in the new or derived creativeness of man himself as seen in all the realms of human experience. Since education is peculiarly the realm in which such creativeness is central, there we should expect to see and can see God's creative working in all learning and all personal transformation to the degree that such learning and transformation are held subordinate to the creative good.

But there is also evil in human existence—human evil for which the individual is responsible (sin) and human evil which is beyond the individual's control. These types of evil are clearly visible in the sphere of education and in the teaching-learning process. We may, therefore, see the redemptive working of God within the sphere of education and in the teaching-learning process as these factors within the process are resisted, judged, transformed, overcome, in whole or in part. We can see the redemptive working of God, for example, in the emergence of truth in the place of error, in the suffering of consequences for the defect or excess of our acts or attitudes, in the discovery of our own pretension or in new insight into our own failure or inadequacy, produced by encounter with a greater good. In all of these we see the "judgment side" of God's redemptive activity. The "healing side" of his redemptive activity is disclosed in the very experience of turning from error or partial truth to a greater truth, in the transformation wrought in us following our awareness of the significance of consequences or of our own failure and inadequacy (a transformation whose character is beyond our direction or control). What the Christian teacher sees happening within the teaching-learning process in a partial or preparatory way or in relation to a segment or aspect of man's existence, he believes will happen in a consummatory and total way as man responds to Christ in faith.

NOTES

CHAPTER II

1. Hoxie N. Fairchild (New York: The Ronald Press, 1952).
2. *Ibid.*, p. 335, in Talcott Parsons' article, "Sociology and Social Psychology."
3. *Ibid.*, ch. ix, "Experimental Psychology."
4. Amos Wilder, *Modern Poetry and the Christian Tradition* (New York: Charles Scribner's Sons, 1952), p. 38.
5. Rupert E. Davies, ed. (New York: The Philosophical Library, 1956), p. 56. Coulson develops this point at length in his *Christianity in an Age of Science* (New York: Oxford University Press, 1953).
6. John Henry Newman, *Historical Sketches,* III (New York: Longmans, Green & Co., 1909), 194.
7. *Systematic Theology,* I (University of Chicago Press, 1951), 12.
8. *The Idea of a University* (New York: Longmans, Green & Co., 1947), p. 310. Used by permission of the publisher.
9. *Ibid.*, p. 44.
10. *Ibid.*, pp. 45-46.
11. *Ibid.*, p. 342.

CHAPTER III

1. *Introductory Papers on Dante* (New York: Harper & Bros., 1955), pp. 101-26.
2. *Keats and Shakespeare* (New York: Oxford University Press, 1924). Quoted in *ibid.*, p. xiii.
3. *Op. cit.*, p. xviii.
4. *T. S. Eliot: Selected Prose,* ed. John Hayward (Harmondsworth, Middlesex: Penguin Books, Ltd., 1955), "Baudelaire," pp. 194, 192.
5. Wilder, *op. cit.*, p. 256.
6. *Ibid.*, p. 259.
7. *Op. cit.*, p. 39.
8. Cf. Cleanth Brooks, "Metaphor and the Function of Criticism," in Stanley Romaine Hopper, *Spiritual Problems in Contemporary Literature* (New York: Harper & Bros., 1952), pp. 131 ff.
9. "The Collaboration of Vision in the Poetic Act" in *Cross Currents,* Spring, 1957, pp. 137-53.
10. Cf. Murray Krieger, *The New Apologists for Poetry* (Minneapolis: University of Minnesota Press, 1956), p. 190.
11. Examples of such analysis of literary works may be found in the books listed in the Selected Readings under the heading "The Christian Teacher and the Humanities."
12. Cf. Hopper, *op. cit.*, p. 130. The phrase is Cleanth Brooks's.
13. *Op. cit.*, p. 54.
14. *On the Limits of Poetry* (New York: William Morrow & Co., 1948), p. 15.
15. Krieger, *op. cit.*, p. 26.
16. (New York: New Directions, 1949). The quotations are chosen from pp. 170-80.
17. All rights reserved. Reprinted by permission of New Directions.
18. *The Saturday Review of Literature,* November 6, 1954, p. 12.
19. Roberts' thesis is developed in an article, "A Christian Theory of Dramatic Tragedy," *The Journal of Religion,* January,

1951, pp. 1-20. The following statements are based on that article.

20. *Ibid.*, p. 20.

21. "Existentialist Aspects of Modern Art" in Carl Michalson, ed., *Christianity and the Existentialists* (New York: Charles Scribner's Sons, 1956), p. 135.

22. *Op. cit.*, I, 235 ff.

23. *Religion in the Making* (New York: The Macmillan Co., 1926), pp. 15-17.

24. *A Psychological Approach to Theology* (New York: Harper & Bros., 1931), pp. 209-12. Used by permission of the publisher.

25. *Three Plays* (London: Martin Secker & Warburg, 1952), p. 27. Used by permission of Hill and Wang, Inc.

26. *Ibid.*, p. 33.

27. *Ibid.*, p. 8.

CHAPTER IV

1. *Personality* (New York: Henry Holt & Co., 1937), p. 308.

2. *Ibid.*, p. 52.

3. *Ibid.*

4. *Ibid.*, p. 213.

5. *Ibid.*, p. 422.

6. *Ibid.*

7. *Explorations in Personality* (New York: Oxford University Press, 1938), pp. 5-11.

8. "Psychology and the Knowledge of Man" in Lewis Leary, ed., *The Unity of Knowledge* (Garden City, N. Y.: Doubleday & Co., 1955), p. 103.

9. *The Use of Personal Documents in Psychological Science* (New York: Social Science Research Council, 1942), chs. iv and xii.

10. *Op. cit.*, pp. 115-16.

11. *Ibid.*, p. 118.

CHAPTER V

1. *The Origins of Modern Science* (London: G. Bell & Sons, 1949), p. viii.
2. *Science and the Modern World* (New York: The Macmillan Co., 1925), p. 3.
3. *Sovereign Reason* (Glencoe, Ill.: The Free Press, 1954), p. 15.
4. *Ibid.* The following paragraphs are based in part on Nagel's excellent introductory essay.
5. For example, cf. Karl Heim, *Christian Faith and Natural Science* (New York: Harper & Bros., 1953), in which Professor Heim discusses the problem of the multiplicity of spaces and the existence of a dimension of reality inaccessible to spatial and temporal measurement. This dimension is inaccessible to measure because all such objectifying methods presuppose this nonobjective ''space'' both logically and chronologically.
6. *Science and the Modern World*, p. 270.
7. *Ibid.*
8. *The Journal of Religion*, April, 1957, pp. 85-98.
9. *Ibid.*, pp. 86, 87.

CHAPTER VI

1. *Education for Modern Man* (New York: Dial Press, 1946), p. 175.
2. *The Light That Flickers* (New York: Harper & Bros., 1947), p. 61.
3. *Op. cit.*, p. 175.
4. *Alma Mater* (New York: Farrar & Rinehart, 1936), p. 107.
5. *The Individual and His Religion* (New York: The Macmillan Co., 1950), p. 31.
6. *The Aims of Education* (New York: New American Library, 1948), p. 18.
7. *The Teaching-Learning Process* (New York: Dryden Press, 1953), p. 79. Cf. also Cantor's *The Dynamics of Learning*

(Buffalo, N. Y.: Foster & Stewart Publishing Corp., 1946).

8. *The Teaching-Learning Process,* p. 8.
9. Sullivan discusses "selective inattention" at length in *The Interpersonal Theory of Psychiatry* (New York: W. W. Norton & Co., 1953) and *Clinical Studies in Psychiatry* (New York: W. W. Norton & Co., 1956).
10. Cambridge, Mass.: Harvard University Press, 1951.
11. *Ibid.,* p. 3. Used by permission of Harvard University Press.
12. *Ibid.,* p. 11.
13. *Ibid.,* p. 7.
14. *Ibid.,* p. 3.
15. "Thought-Processes in Lectures and Discussions," *Journal of General Education,* 1953, 7, 160-69.
16. Joseph Axelrod, Benjamin S. Bloom, *et al., Teaching by Discussion in the College Program* (University of Chicago, 1949).
17. *Ibid.,* p. 15.
18. *Ibid.,* p. 24.

CHAPTER VII

1. Houston Peterson, ed., *Great Teachers* (New Brunswick, N. J.: Rutgers University Press, 1946), pp. 213-14. Used by permission of the publisher.
2. Harold Taylor, ed., *Essays in Teaching* (New York: Harper & Bros., 1950), pp. 178-79.

CHAPTER VIII

1. The following paragraphs are based on a chapter by Robert J. Havighurst, "Who Should Go to College?" in Esther Lloyd-Jones and Margaret R. Smith, *Student Personnel Work as Deeper Teaching* (New York: Harper & Bros., 1954).
2. Robert J. Havighurst, *Human Development and Education* (New York: Longmans, Green & Co., 1953), p. 2.
3. *Ibid.,* p.3.
4. "Growth and Crises of the Healthy Personality" in Milton

J. E. Senn, ed., *Symposium on the Healthy Personality* (New York: Josiah Macy Foundation, 1950), p. 141.

5. *Ibid.*
6. *Ibid.*
7. *Varieties of Human Value* (University of Chicago Press, 1956).
8. Heath has discussed aspects of his Princeton study in three articles appearing in the *Princeton Alumni Weekly:* "55 Who Came to Princeton," Vol. LI, No. 4, October 20, 1950; "Some Comments on the Underclass Years," Vol. LIV, No. 4, October 16, 1953; and "Four Years' Changes," Vol. LVI, No. 5, October 5, 1955.
9. Clements C. Fry, *Mental Health in College* (New York: The Commonwealth Fund, 1942), p. 4.
10. *Ibid.*

CHAPTER IX

1. *Considerations on Personality Development in College Students* by the Committee on the College Student of the Group for the Advancement of Psychiatry, Topeka, Kansas.

CHAPTER X

1. Remark attributed to President A. T. Hadley of Yale in Janet A. Kelley, *College Life and the Mores* (New York: Teachers College, 1949), p. 35.
2. "Autobiographical Notes" in Paul A. Schilpp, ed., *The Philosophy of Alfred North Whitehead,* The Library of Living Philosophers (Evanston, Ill.: Northwestern University, 1941), III, 7.

CHAPTER XI

1. *The Aims of Education,* p. 26.
2. *Concerning the Teacher and On the Immortality of the Soul* (New York: D. Appleton-Century Co., 1938).
3. Cf. Question CXVII, "Of Things Pertaining to the Action of Man," *Summa Theologica,* Part I, in *Basic Writings of Saint*

Thomas Aquinas, ed. Anton C. Pegis (New York: Random House, 1945).

4. *The Story of My Life* (New York: Doubleday, Page & Co., 1909), pp. 22-24, 29-31.

5. *The Source of Human Good* (University of Chicago Press, 1946), p. 56.

6. "Creative Love in Education," *World Christian Education,* IV, Second Quarter, 1949, 27.

7. *Ibid.,* p. 34.

8. *Ibid.*

9. Donald Snygg and Arthur W. Combs, *Individual Behavior* (New York: Harper & Bros., 1949), p. 217. Used by permission of the publisher.

10. Carl Becker, "Frederick Jackson Turner," in Peterson, *op. cit.,* pp. 231-32. Used by permission of Rutgers University Press.

11. *Ibid.,* p. 233.

12. *Ibid.,* pp. 234-35.

13. *Ibid.,* pp. 237-38.

14. *Ibid.,* p. 243.

15. *Between Man and Man,* tr. R. G. Smith (New York: The Macmillan Co., 1948), p. 98. Used by permission of The Macmillan Co. and Routledge & Kegan Paul Ltd.

16. *Ibid.,* p. 98.

17. *Ibid.,* pp. 99-100.

18. *Ibid.,* p. 102.

19. *Ibid.*

20. *Ibid.*

SELECTED READINGS

A large number of books and articles have been published touching on the problems discussed in this book. The following list includes some of the most thought-provoking, any of which might serve as a focus for discussion by groups of concerned teachers or which might simply stimulate the thinking of the individual teacher who wishes to pursue further some of the issues raised in preceding chapters.

THE PROBLEM OF VOCATION

Nelson, John Oliver, ed. *Work and Vocation*. New York: Harper & Bros., 1954.

World Council of Churches Assembly, Evanston, 1954. "The Laity and His Christian Vocation" in *The Christian Hope and the Task of the Church*. New York: Harper & Bros., 1954.

THE CHRISTIAN TEACHER AND HIS DISCIPLINE

Davies, Rupert E., ed. *An Approach to Christian Education*. New York: The Philosophical Library, 1956.

Fairchild, Hoxie N., ed. *Religious Perspectives in College Teaching*. New York: The Ronald Press, 1952.

THE CHRISTIAN TEACHER AND THE HUMANITIES

Hopper, S. R., ed. *Spiritual Problems in Contemporary Literature*. New York: Harper & Bros., 1952.

Jarrett-Kerr, Martin. *Studies in Literature and Belief*. New York: Harper & Bros., 1955.

Scott, Nathan. *Modern Literature and the Religious Frontier*. New York: Harper & Bros., 1958.

————. *Rehearsals of Discomposure*. New York: Columbia University Press, 1952.

————, ed. *Tragic Vision and the Christian Faith*. New York: Association Press, 1957.

Stewart, Randall. *American Literature and Christian Doctrine*. Baton Rouge, La.: Louisiana State University Press, 1958.

Wilder, Amos. *Modern Poetry and the Christian Tradition*. New York: Charles Scribner's Sons, 1952.

THE CHRISTIAN TEACHER AND THE SOCIAL SCIENCES

Butterfield, Herbert. *Christianity and History*. New York: Charles Scribner's Sons, 1950.

Casserley, J. V. L. *Morals and Man in the Social Sciences*. New York: Longmans, Green & Co., 1951.

Hallowell, John H. *Moral Foundation of Democracy*. University of Chicago Press, 1954

Hutchinson, John A., ed. *Christian Faith and Social Action*. New York: Charles Scribner's Sons, 1953.

Niebuhr, Reinhold. *Faith and History*. New York: Charles Sribner's Sons, 1949.

Ward, A. Dudley, ed. *The Goals of Economic Life*. New York: Harper & Bros., 1953.

THE CHRISTIAN TEACHER AND THE NATURAL SCIENCES

Heim, Karl. *Christian Faith and Natural Science*. New York: Harper & Bros., 1957. Torchbooks.

————. *The Transformation of the Scientific World View*. New York: Harper & Bros., 1954.

Smethurst, Arthur F. *Modern Science and Christian Beliefs*. Nashville: Abingdon Press, 1957.

Whitehead, A. N. *Science and the Modern World*. New York: The Macmillan Co., 1925. Ch. xii, "Religion and Science."

ON TEACHERS AND TEACHING

Barzun, Jacques. *Teacher in America*. New York: Doubleday & Co., 1954. Anchor Books.

Fuess, C. M., and Basford, E. S., eds. *Unseen Harvests*. New York: The Macmillan Co., 1949.

Highet, Gilbert. *The Art of Teaching*. New York: Alfred A. Knopf, Inc., 1950.

Peterson, Houston, ed. *Great Teachers*. New Brunswick. N. J.: Rutgers University Press, 1946.

ON COUNSELING

Hiltner, Seward. *The Counselor in Counseling*. Nashville: Abingdon Press, 1952.

Merriam, T. W. *Religious Counseling of College Students*. Washington, D. C.: American Council on Education, 1943.

Outler, Albert C. *A Christian Context for Counseling*. Haddam, Conn.: Hazen Foundation, 1945.

ON THE ACADEMIC COMMUNITY

Brown, Kenneth I. *Not Minds Alone*. New York: Harper & Bros., 1954.

Kelley, Janet A. *College Life and the Mores*. New York: Teachers College, 1949.

Wilson, Logan. *The Academic Man*. New York: Oxford University Press, 1942.

ON COLLEGE STUDENTS

Butz, Otto, ed. *The Unsilent Generation*. New York: Rinehart Co., 1958.

Farnsworth, Dana L. *Mental Health in College and University*. Cambridge, Mass.: Harvard University Press, 1957.

Havemann, Ernest, and West, Patricia. *They Went to College.*

New York: Harcourt, Brace & Co., 1952.

Jacob, Philip E. *Changing Values in College*. New York: Harper & Bros., 1957.

Townsend, Agatha. *College Freshmen Speak Out*. New York: Harper & Bros., 1956.

GENERAL WORKS ON EDUCATION

Harvard Committee. *General Education in a Free Society*. Cambridge, Mass.: Harvard University Press, 1945.

Hutchins, Robert M. *The Higher Learning in America*. New Haven, Conn.: Yale University Press, 1936.

Meland, Bernard E. *Higher Education and the Human Spirit*. University of Chicago Press, 1953.

Moberly, Walter H. *The Crisis in the University*. New York: The Macmillan Co., 1950.

Newman, John Henry. *The Idea of a University*. New York: Longmans, Green & Co., 1947.

Redfield, Robert. *The Redfield Lectures*. Pasadena, Calif.: The Fund for Adult Education, 1955.

Smith, Huston. *The Purposes of Higher Education*. New York: Harper & Bros., 1955.

Whitehead, A. N. *The Aims of Education*. New York: New American Library, 1948.

Wilder, Amos, ed. *Liberal Learning and Religion*. New York: Harper & Bros., 1951.